ROGUES OF RHODE ISLAND

BOBBY O' OLIVEIRA

Omni Publishing Co.

2024

Published by Omni Publishing Co.
www.omni-pub.com

Library of Congress cataloging in publication data
Oliveira, Bobby

Rogues of Rhode Island

ISBN: 978-1-928758-17-4

Printed in the United States of America

DEDICATION

This book is dedicated to my two moms. Sheila O'Brien brought me into the world in the most difficult of situations. Arlene Oliveira guided me through early life and gave me opportunities to experience great things other folks only dream about. Both of them played a role in my sobriety which makes me able to write this now.

ACKNOWLEDGEMENTS

I want to offer thanks to the Faithful Companions of Jesus, the Benedictines, and the Jesuits. Somehow even though I managed to start drinking at 10 and using cocaine at 12, they were able to teach me how to communicate in so many varied ways. Thanks to those lessons, I've campaigned for different presidential candidates in 38 states, was a speech writer for a future Chair of the Massachusetts Democratic Party, changed the Fall River City motto, got to serve as the Sales Director at the Newport Bay Club, helped make the downtown hospital happen up in Utica, and now have written this book. Most importantly, I can talk other people struggling from addiction into recovery. I have done a lot of that in over 21 years. I suppose I should mention I especially want to thank the Jesuits for teaching me some "secret things" that helped make all of those tasks a little bit easier.

TABLE OF CONTENTS

INTRODUCTION

Rhode Island has always been a little off. Some trace it back to when we were the first state to vote on the Constitution and voted no. Others take it further than that when one of our early founders, and idol of mine, Governor Coddington, wanted to have a Civil War with the Massachusetts Bay Colony. This kind of off behavior has attracted many different criminals to Rhode Island as well as created a few.

In Rhode Island Rogues, we will go over some of their histories. There will be no surprise that many mafia members will work their way throughout the chapters. It's always interesting to watch a "wannabe mafia" show on TV and say how it compares to events you may have actually experienced while living in Rhode Island.

We also cannot ignore the role that dark Spirituality plays in Rhode Island. It is one of the reasons Rhode Island Ghost Tours attract so many visitors from other states. It's also one of the reasons that Rhode Island criminals are so creepy.

Best of all, I not only write about the criminals, I describe how I share some qualities with them. Some of them have the same combination of mental illnesses I do, so I can understand their thinking. My life in addiction, more than 21 years sober now, and politics (I'll never be sober from that) has caused me to experience 34 arrests and three indictments. But thanks to great lawyers, I had only eight convictions, without ever having to snitch. I even ran my own refined cocaine product enterprise in Massachusetts for a little while, so yeah, I get where some of these folks are coming from. That makes it easier to make their behaviors relatable on an everyday basis.

OVERVIEW

I think I may have been five years old when I first heard a "personality" on AM radio glorify a Rhode Island criminal. If you ever wonder what radio sounded like when I was growing up, when folks weren't talking, just listen to Yacht Rock. In between the songs, there would be discussions of celebrities. In Rhode Island, a good number of them were criminals. First to burn down the Gaspee, first to reject the Constitution via vote; maybe it makes sense.

I had this reinforced during the Claus Von Bulow trial. At the time that happened, my mother was a part owner of the Coiffure-Sur-Mer salon. It's now a bed and breakfast. Going to private schools and having both parents working in Newport has its advantages. Even though some of the celebrities wouldn't show up in the actual case until later on, such as Alan Dershowitz, I would meet them daily between the courthouse and the salon. While constantly being reminded by "caring adults" that some of the encounters I was having were with "bad people," it was hard to avoid because all the bad people had the better personalities.

While all that is happening, the mafia was being "storified" out of context. I judge everything organized crime wise against that time in 1990, when I first got invited to visit Whitey Bulger in the garage. When I was a kid, you would meet every person connected to the mob; for some reason, my parents enjoyed the same restaurants they did, so a lot of introductions – many in men's rooms – met that standard. In the last 10 years, having mob leadership run out of Boston was the first clue, it hasn't actually stood up. Right now, the Rhode Island mob isn't even on the Utica or Albany levels.

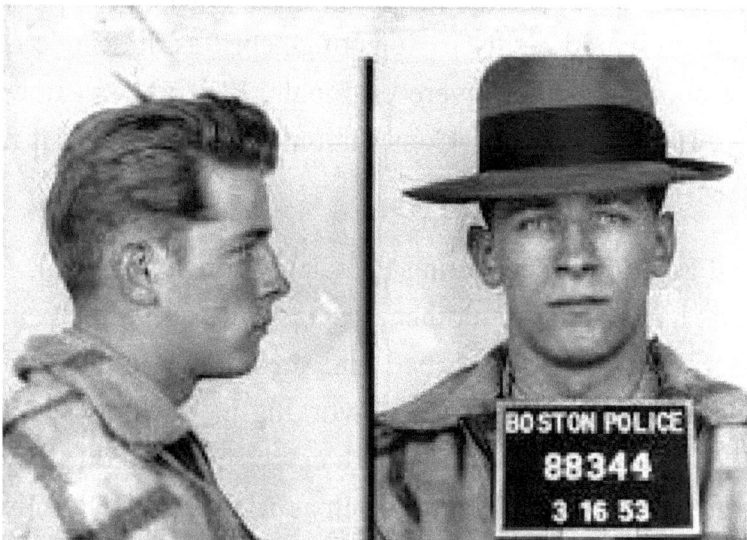

WHITEY BULGER MUG SHOT

From first through sixth grade, going to school meant driving over the Sakonnet Bridge to get to Saint Philomena's. In ninth grade, it meant driving over that same bridge to get to Portsmouth Abbey. Funny thing about going to school on Aquidneck Island – teachers feel the need to remind you daily that you're on an island. That means they'll talk about the bridges. If I wasn't adopted down in Key West and moved here, I wouldn't know how many crimes found their origins on bridges. My birth family members were key players in the West Palm Beach Kennel Club. I would know how many crimes are connected to dog tracks instead.

When I was 18, I got a job giving tours at Astor's Beechwood, in character no less. During the day, Charles Thurston Sedgewick the fifth – friends called him Chuck 5 – would lead tourists around the Mansion. At night, I would find the bars that would serve me drinks without an ID because I worked at a mansion. "Wanna come see my mansion?" worked more than once, sad to say. After sleeping at the mansion, we'd get up early and go "jogging with Senator Pell." This weird community jog thing is where you learned about all the naughtiness rich people were into, as they described what happened from the night before.

I thought that was bad enough. In 2001 at the start of my timeshare career, I moved back to the city yet again. Now I had access to the folks who spent a lot of money to live in a resort for a week. They had even better stories to tell about the rich and famous roaming around Rhode Island, and not exactly following the rules.

You should be aware that I do suffer from Narcissistic Personality Disorder. My parents found out when I was doing "serial killer things" as a five-year-old. I also suffer from the Dark Triad. It was really bad until I got sober; the symptoms rolled back a lot but they're still there waiting to be discovered. When I go into deep detail about some of the criminal acts, you might cringe. Inside somewhere, due to my collection of mental illnesses, I might be smiling just a little. That may explain when I delight so much in the details. Just wanted you to be forewarned.

"Mike Stanton is our preeminent aficionado and raconteur of Rhode Island's flamboyantly criminal political follies, and The Prince of Providence is the chronicle of a great American rogue, Mayor Buddy Cianci – a paragon of charisma and corruption."

– Philip Gourevitch, Author

WHAT ATTRACTS US TO CRIMINALITY?

It is usually a two-fold answer. On one hand, none of us really likes following the rules. We do it so we get a reward. Then we see the people who don't and they sometimes appear – key word "appear" – happier. The second side is our fascination with death. That's why the ghost tours I do are so popular. Everyone wants to know what it is like being at that exact point in the universe when someone travels from one side to the other, without actually crossing it themselves.

As cool as the Mafia is, they sometimes miss out on the second part. Drug gangs and mafia types can come across like the Louisville shooter comes across this morning. Lots of big bang but little of that creepy side. It's almost boorish.

Folks in Rhode Island are further drawn to this for a couple of reasons. Rhode Island's history is kind of like my own. For me, it was being the product of incest and rape, being given up for adoption, all while having some awesome talents but paralyzing mental illnesses at the same time. For Rhode Island, it was splitting off from Massachusetts, almost having its own Civil War, burning down the Gaspee, but still voting against the Constitution the first time it gets presented. We are a problem child.

The water plays into this too. Death is connected to water, which is one of the things that makes sailing so amazing. There you are using only the wind and tug of a rope to take a ride over where so many others have died. Boat sinkings are always memorialized, even when it's just a disappearance and not a sinking like the Sea Bird story. It happened on the water so we can all recite it.

Through that criminal element, especially a potential criminal like Doris Duke, the Rough Point story becomes gold. By the way, if you don't believe that she did it, head down there around 3 am. Ghosts don't like drunken tourist hours, and ask the entities still hanging around. They'll tell you she did it, her money let her get away with it, and the story will always have value especially since each time it gets told, the water is in the background.

I also suppose part of this is our own Judeo-Christian version of death. "Ok, so you die, then you wake, and there will be an old guy sitting there with a book that wants to review your life" just can't be the whole story. That has to be especially true for the criminal types, who will be asked, "So when you shot the store clerk over the price of a handle of Vodka, what were you thinking?" There has to be so much more to go over in depth. If that's the whole process, why not be a little wilder?

Death Called Accident For Heiress' Friend

NEWPORT, R. I., Oct. 10.—(UPI)—The death of Eduardo Tirella, who was knocked against a gate by an automobile driven by Doris Duke, tobacco heiress, was an apparent "'unfortunate accident," police said today.

Police Chief Joseph A. Radice said Miss Duke told police she and Tirella were going out to dinner Friday and he was driving.

HE STOPPED 10 to 15 feet in front of the gate on her estate and got out to open the huge iron gates. She said she slid over to the driver's seat to drive through the gate after it was opened.

"All she can remember is that the car sped forward and that he was standing in the center of the gate," Radice said.

Radice said the investigation was continuing and police were awaiting a complete autopsy report. Miss Duke's lawyer, Wesley N. Nash of New York City, was present during the question-

—A. P. wirephoto.
EDUARDO TIRELLA

ing yesterday, Radice said.

WHEN ASKED, "Does this appear to be an unfortunate accident?" Radice answered "Yes."

Tirella, 42, a designer had been a constant companion of Miss Duke for the past decade.

Yesterday Newport police questioned Miss Duke, 53, who was hospitalized after the accident with facial injuries and shock. She was released from the hospital on Saturday, but was not questioned at that time because of a request by her physi-

NEWS COVERAGE OF DORIS DUKE "ACCIDENT"

For me, it's always been about cemeteries. I didn't know why as a kid, other than to think I could somehow connect with my birth mom because I knew nothing about her. Then I learned as a sober person that trips to the cemetery meant I "learned" things I didn't know before. Was I interacting with ghosts? What about that time at the former asylum when I talked to that woman, walked into the next room to tell the staff about the cool person I met, and they said, "Oh yeah, she's been dead for 37 years." It's a natural progression to want to learn about who made people ghosts in the first place.

With every issue, there is a back door. Some folks are not into any of these things but just want to pursue justice for victims. Cold case podcast numbers are off the charts. All they want to do is discover who did the murder. They take a look at the evidence and want it to compare to other criminal "signatures." In order to do that, they have learned a number of other criminal signatures, which means learning about a bunch of criminals. Before they know it, they are entirely sucked into the criminal universe. Would a couple of examples help?

Back in May of 2022, there was a serial rapist running around Providence. The dark net came to life and exposed another breaking and entering person. The signatures were close. Turns our breaking and entering person and rape guy were not the same humans. The dark net didn't know that and encouraged violence against the breaking and entering guy. Yes, he committed crimes but not rape crimes. The dark almost got him killed, according to some friends spending time at the ACI, because their criminal research told them he was somebody he wasn't.

Then there's the serial killer I will get into later. All I will say for now is that he decided serial killing was his thing by watching the Sopranos. It spun him off into another direction, and before he knew it, he was at the local hardware store buying tools. Not because he had a lousy childhood, not to get over pain, but because the Sopranos TV show caused him to do research on criminals.

While you're attracted to the criminals' abilities to ignore society's rules, you may root for them. I ask you to do one thing as you go through this book. Ask your Higher Power, or the universe itself if you don't have one, to bring peace to the victims. They did have to suffer in order for you to enjoy the stories now, just like ghosts have to continually suffer so people can see them now.

Parts of what you are about to read will outrage you. Some of what you're about to read will make you smile, only to yourself, and hear, "Hey, why can't I do that?" in your head. As a Bipolar person, I'm not going to judge what anyone hears in their own head. Within a short amount of time, you will discover which kind of criminals make you the happiest. Maybe that is something you should reflect on.

NICHOLAS ALAHVERDIAN

Not for nuthin', but I thought my 34 arrests, three indictments, and eight convictions, while never having to snitch, was kind of impressive. This guy I'm about to tell you about got arrested after he was dead. That's some effort Nicholas Alahverdian put in.

Not surprisingly, Nicholas grew up in an abusive household. His parents were alcoholics and there might have been some drug use. Every time one of us in the adopted community gets angry at our adopted parents, we should always be reminded what our birth parents could have been like.

Nicholas was placed by DCYF with another family. He had Narcissistic Personality Disorder, Attention Deficit Disorder, and probably Oppositional Defiant Disorder – also known as "Jerk's disease." Ok, so the word isn't "jerk" but you get the idea. He was constantly yelling at his foster parents and throwing things at them. His brothers and sisters weren't safe. As a result, he spent a great deal of time in the "behavioral modification unit" at Butler hospital. Psychiatric care would become a regular thing. It got so bad, he spent a year and a half in DCYF's "night-to-night" program.

What is the night-to-night program? That's where you spend the day at a DCYF building, probably in Pawtucket, and the night in various homeless shelters. It's a great way to get bullied and have all your stuff taken. During this period, Nicholas was not attending school. I've talked to people in recovery who went through this experience. It is indeed spirit crushing.

NICHOLAS ALAHVERDIAN

If that weren't weird enough, Nicholas says he was sent to Boys Town in Nebraska at age 16. This is true even though he was a Rhode Island General Assembly Page at 14 and at 15 claimed to form an organization, which he hadn't, called Nexus Government.

A year later at 17, he was sent to a Florida program where kids regularly had a terrible time. You know things are bad if DCYF ends their contract with you. Nicholas claims he was beaten continuously, by staff and others, for three years. While Nicholas often has problems with the truth, this is probably on the money.

From 2006 to 2008, things got weirdly quiet. Then magically he shows up in Ohio. There are rumors that he has already formed an early version of the Incel movement online. One day at Sinclair College, he pins a young lady up against the wall. According to the police report, she's not really there to be touched. Besides the pressure he uses to keep her in this spot, his other hand is masturbating while telling her how beautiful she looks.

This incident is going to show up a lot. He will end up with a sex offender status out of it. In the future, he will be thrown out of classes at Harvard due to that status. He is going to file many lawsuits over this incident and lose them all. Then he will write a book where he will claim this was his "Personal 911."

He's not close to done. Somehow he has a house in Utah. He's constantly driving women to it, failing to get laid, and then threatening them. In the summer 2010, he practically kidnapped a young lady in Pawtucket. He soon realizes kidnapping could be a problem. That winter he pulls the same stunt but this time makes the young lady read a disclaimer that he videotaped.

Do you remember where you were on November 11, 2010? If you were Nicholas, you were beating up a girlfriend. She screams so loud that another woman calls in the cops. When they arrive, the girlfriend has obviously taken a beating and they arrest Nicholas. Nicholas responds by smashing his own head in the cop car. The cops pepper spray him trying to get him to calm down.

In 2011, he launched a series of lawsuits against DCYF. They got settled in August, 2013. All we know for sure is a $200,000 lien was waived. The case never went to trial and an agreement was reached. Later on that year, he got married. That will last a whole six months. No contact orders and assault accusations abound.

In 2017, a friendship is going to go about as well. He will move in with a friend in Providence. The friend will soon discover that Nicholas has grabbed the friend's checkbook and is on a spree. More cops, more no-contact orders, another disappearance.

During this time, he is lobbying many Rhode Island legislators about DCYF. The one idea that comes forward dies in committee. Legislators will later say that he was already asking them for cash. When they wouldn't come through, Nicholas would make claims about knowing women they had supposedly raped. Every legislator that came in contact with him found the whole thing draining.

In 2019, he meets a woman that will cause him to get married again. This time in England. He has changed his hair and his name.

Right after the marriage, he suddenly has non-Hodgkins Lymphoma. He's not living in the United States, supposedly, but news of his death is spread all over the country.

Law enforcement is not having any of this. They were motivated by the fact that Nicholas had never registered as he was supposed to due to the Ohio "masturbate while holding a woman against a wall" incident. Different people claiming to be Nicholas's widow would show up from time to time. Sometimes requesting a Mass, sometimes sending an email, sometimes calling the media. All of them were obviously fake and in some cases might have been Nicholas himself.

In February 2021, an Irish reporter filed a public records request. Nobody by Nicholas's name had a death certificate recorded. In December, he caught COVID. While getting treatment at a hospital, the Scottish Police picked him up. The guy calling himself Arthur Knight had tattoos that matched the guy who used to call himself Nicholas Rossi, who turned out to be the plain old Nicholas the whole time.

It didn't take long to discover that Nicholas had no lung issues. He had a thing for faking seizures and all the doctors and nurses knew. It was now also becoming clearer that the "Louise" sending all the emails and making calls with fake voices, when Nicholas wasn't doing it, was the wife he had divorced after just six months of marriage. We can only imagine what her issues are like.

He would have been extradited by now, but guess what? More rape allegations have surfaced and Scottish Police want to investigate those first. Much like in the old "night-to-night" program days, fellow prisoners are supposedly having a hell of a time with him as we speak. You know if he ever gets through this part and gets sent back here to the US, he's going to be desperate right? What a shame if he gives up just horrible information about a Rhode Island legislator but we can't believe it because it came from Nicholas. Maybe getting arrested after you die is overrated.

NICKY BIANCO

The thing that 20-something-year-old me misses about Nicky Bianco the most is that he was normal. He was likable. When you met him, you thought he was cool. It never failed. You'd be drinking somewhere up on the hill after finally coming of age. You'd run into a politician you had interned for somewhere along the way. Nicky was hanging with some of his friends and he'd come by to say "hi" to the politician who would then ask, "Have you met Mr. Bianco before"? Nicky would tell a joke or quip about a young lady's attractiveness and be off on his way. Kind of like one of your uncles.

Nicky was literally born and raised on Federal Hill. He grew up like a lot of us did - except for the fact he had relatives in the mob. Along the way, he learned to appreciate the value of education. You know because of how he educated his own kids.

He also knew how to reach out to those in authority. In his late twenties and early thirties, he had moved to Brooklyn and was part of the Colombo crime family. The Colombos were on the brink of a civil war. It was Nicky who reached out to Raymond Patriarca, Sr. and said, "Can you put together some order and a settlement here"? He knew enough to ask for that help, and had the guts to follow through, at 31 years of age. I wasn't even sober at 31.

NICKY BIANCO

In 1982, Anthony Mirabella was guilty of numerous "code violations." Not only was he not behaving, he was not listening to those trying to get him back on track. Depending on who you believe, Nicky planned the Mirabella shooting or at least signed off on it. The cool part is Nicky always played it soft and smooth. That is one of the reasons he stopped living on Atwells Avenue and moved to Barrington. He never let his ego get in the way. You can't find his voice recorded anywhere because he was careful. For that reason, he was acquitted at the Mirabella trial.

Right after that, Raymond Patriarca, Sr. passes away and Ray Jr. takes over. What a freaking mess. Hard to believe the Rhode Island mob would later be in worse shape, compared to the state of things today. They were still awesome in this period, but "ego satisfaction" was clearly getting in the way of "business." The family is pretty much having a civil war with itself and its own crew in Boston. Meanwhile, other Massachusetts crews, on a really minor level, are showing no respect whatsoever. Nicky is doing whatever he can just to keep a semblance of things together.

In 1985, Nicky was accused of setting up the hit on Richard Callei. Once again, Nicky's quiet style of living pays off. The Prosecution can't put enough evidence against him and the charges are dismissed.

The Providence versus Boston thing came to a head in 1989. William "Wild Guy" Grasso gets killed by some Massachusetts types. He was kind of the boss. It should be noted that running around with the nickname "Wild Guy" because of what you did in strip clubs tells us everything you need to know about him. Never before had so many lap dances been interrupted. Ray Junior is trying to run things but Nicky is really the boss at this time.

In 1989, Ray Junior screwed Nicky over. Depending on what version of the story you believe, Ray Junior goes to a Patriarca family "admission event." They did such a lousy job setting it up that they don't notice the FBI has infiltrated with surveillance equipment. Also, there is John F. "Sonny" Castagna. He will eventually turn government witness. He will also inform Ray Jr. that if he doesn't fully step aside right after the indictment that the Boston crew plans to kill them.

Thanks to Sonny's turning snitch and Ray Junior's incompetence, Nicky gets indicted in 1990. Being as careful as all get out does not help you when one of your "friends" in the room decides their chances at freedom matter more than you do. Nicky ends up getting convicted in Hartford, Connecticut, of all places, in August 1991. Just before Thanksgiving 1991, he will be sentenced to 11 years of federal time.

Sadly, he will not complete the sentence. Somewhere along the way, he developed ALS. He died while serving time in Missouri.

JOHN BRIGGS

You used to be able to get away with a lot more stuff. This was especially true if you captured the moment. John Briggs did exactly that – at the White Horse Tavern in Newport no less.

In 1673, Rebecca Cornell was found burned to death. Could barely tell it was her. In fact, if it hadn't happened in her bedroom, people may have guessed it was somebody else. Folks thought it was just an accident.

48 hours after she gets buried, John Briggs, her brother, is asleep. She shows up in his dream. He has no clue of what's happening and screams out. She tells him who she is.

He thinks his deceased sister's appearance was her way of saying she was murdered, and that her son Thomas did it. How did he get from point A to point B? Nobody knows. They re-inspect the body and find a wound to the stomach. Based on the testimony of a ghost, in this case "ghost hearsay," the jury convicts Thomas

29

Cornell and sentences him to death.

WHITE HORSE TAVERN, NEWPORT, RI

Today, people say his ghost still roams between Washington Square and the White Horse Tavern. I have no idea if John Briggs had anything to do with the original murder, but if there was a beef between him and Mr. Cornell, Briggs pulled it off nicely. Yes, Mr. Cornell is Lizzie Borden's granddaddy. Yes, I got sober in the house behind the White Horse Tavern. Yes, those two items helped John Briggs make the list.

DENNYS CABRERA

Back in the late nineties, I used to be a refined cocaine product entrepreneur. I never carried a weapon. The Army taught me how to, I just never did. None of my crew ever did unless they were on a "money laundering" run. I only had weapons pointed at me when I bought a couple of kilos for "refined product creation."

When I went to Utica in 2013, the mob there was following a "violence only when necessary" motto. Same for the mobsters I've met in New York City. Whitey tried to hold up that motto but too many of his crew were living in addiction. The point is, once you establish what you'll do if somebody steps out of bounds, the need for senseless violence goes way down. Gangs never practice this rule.

That's what makes the Dennys Cabrera story that much more annoying. He couldn't get access to a party. Access to a freaking party is all that was at stake.

Instead of just taking the "L" or trying to buy his way in, Dennys takes out a firearm. Nairobi Acosta was the doorman on Baxter Street that night. He would die from his injuries. Imagine having to explain that to his family?

However, the fireworks weren't over. Mr. Cabrera decided the crowd should feel his pain, so he shot indiscriminately into a group of people. Claudio Neves was just hanging outside and got injured for no reason that night.

DENNYS CABRERA

After the shooting, Dennys took off and he's still on the run. He hadn't even built up enough cred to have a cool nickname. Killed one guy, hurt another, and then fled knowing he could never use his real name again.

Some folks theorize he's in New York City but all my friends down there say they've never seen him or heard of him on the streets. He is originally from the Dominican Republic, so he may have headed back there. I know it doesn't happen a lot, but if someone leaves your nation, commits a crime, flees, and heads back where home originally was, how does that make the local government feel?

Right now, there are approximately 26 gangs in Providence. Between associates and members, we're talking about 1,600 kids. I say kids because the average age is 15. About 190,000 people live in Providence, of whom 21,000 are school-aged kids, to keep the numbers in perspective.

Yes, we can talk about mental illness and how mental illness leads to addiction. However, there is something else going on here. Mental illness and addiction alone, or having parents suffering from those issues, does not explain shooting into a crowd because you can't get into a party. Something else is at play and we need to discover what that is and how to fix it.

Bobby Oliveira

BUDDY CIANCI

It's sad when what you see might be the last of something. A criminal with style, a sense of humor, and the ability to tell harsh truths in a nice way has become a rare art form. It used to be the way things worked. Buddy Cianci not only broke the mold, but in numerous ways caused the mold makers to go on an extended vacation.

Buddy grew up in Cranston. At age seven, he was appearing on WJAR's weekend Kiddie Revue show. He ended up going to Moses Brown School and becoming roommates with Adrian Hendricks, the first black kid to attend the school. He would get a Bachelor's degree at Fairfield, a Masters at Villanova, and his Juris Doctor at Marquette University Law School. Throughout his political career, he was offered honorary degrees by numerous Rhode Island colleges and universities, including Johnson and Wales and Roger Williams University.

Buddy always had good timing. He got the gig as a Special Assistant Attorney General in 1969. That meant in 1972, when Italian folks were being portrayed as siding with criminals all the time, he was part of the team working for the state against Raymond Patriarca, Sr. For the record, Ray, Sr., also had qualities we haven't seen in a while. Buddy would continue to investigate corruption in government and gained quite the reputation.

BUDDY CIANCI

In 1974, thanks to in part an internal Democratic Party revolt, Buddy became Mayor of Providence the first time. Irish folks had been mayor for 150 years before then. Buddy liked attending things. Backyard barbeques, store openings, little league playoff games, weddings and carnivals all worked for Buddy. He had the right personality. He got made fun of due to his willingness to attend these events, but that's how many of us met him. We caught onto his personality right away.

Buddy always wanted to be more than mayor. He got to address the 1976 Republican Convention, and mentions of him for Vice President got into his head. He would run for both governor and senator and lose both. Looking back, one of his huge problems was that while he had the personality, he didn't have the campaign cash or the field workers outside of the city to make it happen. Beyond the desire to achieve, constant battling over the municipal budget could not have been that exciting.

You're surprised that even though he was "socially liberal" Buddy was a Republican? This happens a lot in Italian political culture. In the Utica version, the mob takeover of the city prevents the south strategy from ever coming to life. Democrats there are a lot closer to the 1964 version, while the Republican Party is more like John Chafee. Here in Rhode Island, we have people who are socially liberal but want the church to support them so they take Republican stands, even though many have paid for abortions. But the Republican Party is a joke so they put "Ds" in front of their names to get elected. Confused yet?

Buddy had to resign from his first term when the Raymond DeLeo incident happened. The story was that Mr. DeLeo had had an affair with Mrs. Cianci and Buddy wanted to engage in revenge. Both Mr. DeLeo and Mrs. Cianci denied the affair happened. Word on the street at the time was that Mrs. Cianci was engaged in numerous affairs while Buddy had the lady of the week now and again. The whole DeLeo thing was a mafia matter. Yes, what parents tell exclusive private school kids, who tell other exclusive private school kids, is the equivalent of "word on the street."

Joe Paolino, a great guy who has taught me a lot, including giving me the job of Field Coordinator for Bill Clinton's RI Presidential Primary Campaign, won the special election to become mayor. Buddy became a talk show host. Thanks to his personality, he was more effective than most, but politics was still his calling.

In 1991, he became Mayor of Providence for the second time. He had an epiphany regarding tourism. He became one of the most "pro art" mayors in the country. The Providence Bruins, the Providence Place shopping mall and the Fleet Skating Center were all part of this new commitment.

If people are coming to stay, they need to eat. Known as an Italian city, if Italian food is not an everyday food for some of the tourists, they will probably want to try some. That's when the "Mayor's Own Marinara Sauce" appeared. While the sauce was great, money laundering meant that it never reported any profits. Trust me, what I bought alone in 2012 should have made them more than the three dollars in profit they reported.

Buddy's second term came to an end because Director of Administration Frank Corrente got caught taking bribes. As usual, when an administration is that sloppy it comes down to a personal issue. Most personal issues tend to be dark.

According to a few sex workers in the city – a couple I worked with in recovery, one I dated before finding out she was a sex worker – Buddy had a sex addiction. Mr. Corrente was taking bribes so Buddy could afford his dates and afford sex workers when dates weren't available. Had he gotten help, he might still be mayor.

Buddy had a thing for making his women happy. If you believe one young lady, he had the Roger Williams Park Zoo opened up one night so they could have sex in the limo in front of the giraffes' cage. I didn't know having giraffes watch you was a thing.

This brings up another uncomfortable subject. Wherever I have been and have dealt with organized crime – be it Fall River, Newport, Whitey's crew in Boston, the traditional gang in Utica, the made guys in New York City – all of them had side chicks. In each case, the young lady knew the guy had a wife and family but just went along with the arrangement anyway, just for the fun of it. In Rhode Island, the mobsters are constantly engaging in transactional sex. Never forget that the day Senate President Ruggerio stole the condoms, he only did so because a young lady was trading sex for a political favor. While I support sex workers, it's not something I've engaged in. Somehow taking the "possibility of failure" out of the whole thing ruins the energy. Once again, that may be why the Providence mob is run out of Boston now.

Buddy would spend five years in prison. Then just two months after being released he had a radio gig. Then a TV gig. Then cartoons were using him as a character. The interesting part was many of us followed his advice, but would never admit where we got it.

In 2014, the election bug bit again. He would lose this time. As it turned out, he would soon be diagnosed with colon cancer. He died in early 2016. He did get two days in an open casket inside Providence City Hall. I just wish more politicians would use him as a guide for personality and communication, leaving aside the sex addiction part.

JAMES DEWOLF

Some people just have their game together. They start out early on their own and before long, they've got their own routines to produce success. James DeWolf, James D'Wolf to his boys, hit the seas at age 13. Back in the day, ships carried arms to defend against pirates. James got his start on this kind of shipping vessel. Even though he got into several conflicts and was captured by the British twice, he hung in there.

When the Revolutionary War ends, James has reached the status of captain even though he's only in his twenties. He decides that the slave trade will be his thing. Yes, Rhode Island did outlaw slave trading in 1787. However, anyone who knows about the history of Newport realizes that didn't mean much.

He's going to be so good at gaming the system, he will eventually get away with a murder. According to the legend, he discovers on one of his ships a young female slave with smallpox. He gets indicted in Rhode Island for having her lowered over the side and into the bay to drown. The process is slow so he decides to run off to St. Thomas, where the case is then heard because he is living there. James testifies that the slave had to be thrown off the ship to protect the health of everyone else on board. The Danish folks in St. Thomas declare him "not guilty."

JAMES DEWOLF

Based on the numbers, James and his family transported close to 12,000 slaves. He was heavily into the rum trade, so you can guess he did the "trade infant slaves for their weight in molasses instead of cash" thing. The family soon figured out that trading slaves was only part of the business. Within two decades, they had a bank, an insurance company that insured slave voyages, and their own slave trading depot in South Carolina.

James would take this knowledge into the war of 1812, where he discovered the coffee and sugar trades. He had a Privateering contract with the United States government, so his ships could go out and mess with the British any time they liked. One of his boats, the Yankee, captured 50 British ships and put up $5 million of earnings. That would be almost $1 billion today. Understanding that there's more to the business than what happens at sea, he helped found the Arkwright Mills. Let's see - most of the mills are in the north, the cotton-picking exercise is a southern thing. No, this won't be a problem at all in the 1860s.

Every so often, James needed to get off the boat and do some "land things." His favorite was to serve in the Rhode Island House of Representatives. He would also become a United States Senator.

Somehow, even though he was constantly on and off the boat, he and his wife Nancy have 12 kids. Maybe DNA tests are in order unless we want to conclude his sperm is as efficient as his slave trading. When he died in 1837, he was the second richest man in the U.S. I've been by his grave in Bristol and never thought about that. What he did, when you get down to it, was disgusting. The way he went about it and outperformed everyone else, however, was amazing.

Bobby Oliveira

DORIS DUKE

Sometimes having connections comes in handy. This is especially true if you might have killed somebody. Doris Duke played this incident well.

On October 7, 1966, Doris Duke smashed Eduardo Tirella with a two-ton station wagon. He died. The weird part is that she actually hit him twice. She claimed that the accident was caused by brake failure. How convenient that he was up against the iron gates at the time. Because she was connected to folks in the Attorney General's Office the way she was, she got away with it.

Looking back, photos and other evidence tell a different story. Doris did have a history of having a few drinks and getting violent. Ask one of her ex-husbands. She also had a history of being rather possessive. Ask anybody she dated.

Problem number one was that his injuries were in the wrong spots to corroborate her story about an accidental brake malfunction causing him to be crushed against the gates. His injuries were up around his skull. The next problem was that Eduardo's blood was found underneath the car. No skin or blood was found on the gates.

ROUGH POINT MANSION, THE NEWPORT HOME OF DORIS DUKE

The theory many journalists have is that she drove intentionally at him. He jumps up on the hood for a second then rolls off. She finishes the job by driving over his head.

This is not to say that outside of this incident she wasn't a good human. Like Alfred Vanderbilt, she inherited cash at an early age, which can cause its own type of problems.

I myself grew up in a family that wasn't exactly rich, but they could afford to send me to private school and go on frequent family vacations. And, it's not as if I never used family connections to get out of things in the past.

There was the night I was driving the wrong way on Route 6 in Seekonk, and the police officer didn't arrest me because he knew one of my cousins. There was a night at SMU, now UMass-Dartmouth, when just dropping my buddy's mom's name got my friends and me off the hook. It's just I never murdered someone or used my connections to get away with it.

Bobby Oliveira

ADAM EMERY

It's nice when the stories I tell during Ghost Tours and the Rogues overlap. Because I'm in Newport, we have to talk about the number of jumpers off the bridge. There are about four or five a year. Each time it happens, orbs can be seen the next day at the famous Wave Statue. In the last seven years or so, homeless folks have reported orbs at the Wave Statue after every drowning. We had a jumper two Sundays before I wrote this. I don't even know if he died but there were orbs at the Wave Statue.

When I get done with that, I get to tell the Adam Emery story. Back in 1990, long enough ago that I was still a speechwriter on Beacon Hill, Adam and his wife were in Warwick leaving a restaurant by Rocky Point. His car was sideswiped. He jumped out of his car with a knife, stabbing and killing the two people in the car that had sideswiped him.

It took him eight months to get released on bail. After that, he turned down several deals and planned to plead self-defense. There was only one problem. According to paint analysis, the car carrying the people he killed was not the same car that had side-swiped him. That's right, he killed the wrong people.

He was out on bail awaiting sentencing that could have been up to 25 years, but he never showed up. People remember seeing him at a sporting goods store and that was it. Three days later, his car was found on the Newport Bridge. It was empty. Two weeks after that, a local fisherman caught a leg in one of his nets. The leg was DNA tested and was a match for Adam's wife. Adam has never been located.

ADAM EMERY

People have seen him in Connecticut. People have seen him in Florida. Some think he ran to France. Many members of the FBI who believe he is alive think he is hanging with family in Italy. It's amazing how few people believe he is dead, even though he was declared so over a decade ago.

If that wasn't annoying enough to families of the victims, including his wife, some of those "catch the crook" reality TV shows have made him a star in some places. At some point we have to discuss, based on how few perps get caught compared to the number of families who have their faces rubbed in it, whether those shows are worth it from an advertising perspective. By all rights, you have the ability to say what you like provided you don't violate hate speech restrictions. But should you be able to monetize it when it's not in the interests of those who have suffered the most?

RONALD FISCHER

It's sad when various television programs create a media star out of someone truly despicable. Rapist Ronald Fischer has become exactly that. I think we're up to five shows on him.

No real genius here. He came from a family with cash. Then he discovered women would respond to personal ads. Once on the date, he'd say, "Wanna see my boat?" Then he'd take them on board The Sea Lion and rape them. In all honesty, when I lived at Astors Beechwood as an 18-year-old kid, I used the "Wanna see my mansion?" line a million times that summer. The difference was I never raped anybody.

By the way, I don't have to say alleged rapist because he pleaded to a previous sexual assault before the current run. The pattern and practice were already there. Tell me if you have heard this before. He was on trial for another rape, this time in Newport, and he just took off. No one respects bail any longer.

One interesting thing about Ronald is that on his fake ID, he used his actual birthday but listed himself as 10 years younger. I suppose that might fool someone during dinner, but if you haven't been taking care of yourself, well by the end of the night she's going to know. Then again, he could have Bipolar 1 like me. Being younger sexually – google "hypomania sexuality" – is one of our magic powers.

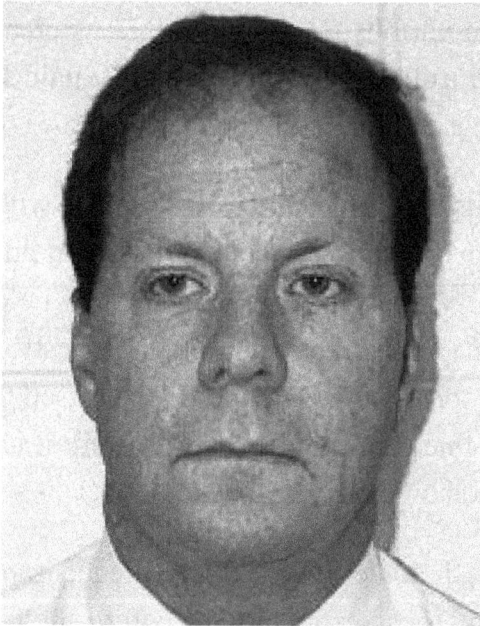

RONALD FISCHER

I also find it interesting that numerous records list his place of birth as Guatemala. Is he adopted like me? Was there an affair in the backstory? Were mom and dad just on a cruise while she was nine months pregnant? All of that must figure into this somehow.

He was indeed educated and worked as an anesthesiologist. You can't tell me he didn't use that during the rapes. Maybe even worse, he may have used those skills to cover them up. You thought you were on a date with Ronald and you woke up behind a 7/11. Your clothes aren't the way they're supposed to be, but everything up to then is a blur. You feel kind of hungover but don't remember drinking.

If he thought he had to rape women in order to have sex, is there any way that stopped? The whole time he was on the run, he must have been raping, right? He already had 11 aliases. What would stop him from picking up a couple of more in states where daddy had connections so the rape-a-thon could continue?

I am the product of what happens when a 13-year-old has a relationship with a 34-year-old. It gets better: they were brother and sister. I was adopted by an upper middle class family and got spoiled a lot. Once I found out how I was created, I had to find out what mom went through. Now I know. It makes me dislike a whole set of people even more. As it stands, over 60 percent of us who are adopted are Pro Choice. Our hatred for rape, and messing with women's body autonomy in general, will always be legendary. I haven't cared up to now, but I hope Ronald gets caught and goes back to trial.

RAYMOND LASSOR

I don't know what caused Raymond Lassor to become a drifter and male sex worker who would murder people. I suppose the biggest clue is that he referred to himself as "self-programmed." It would appear the only way he could reduce the pain he was feeling was by taking it out on someone else.

He changed a lot of things in Rhode Island. He made it clear that serial killers could happen here as well. He might have also changed the way we looked at our own laws.

We do know about four victims. In all likelihood, there were more. My parents sent me to the shrink at age five when I was doing "serial killer things." I was diagnosed with Narcissistic Personality Disorder. I had multiple adventures before they found out what I was up to.

Lori Carlucci was a local prostitute familiar to some. She was found on June 27, 1984, strangled and only partially clothed in downtown Providence. She was left in a vacant parking lot.

57

In August it would be Wanda Sue Adams' turn. An aspiring model who had Gospel singing talent, she was in Providence visiting family. She would be found floating, once again strangled and barely clothed, in the Woonasquatucket River.

RAYMOND LASSOR

The last murder was discovered at the end of the month. 58-year-old Delores Neuser was discovered in a parking garage. By now, everybody is freaking and a task force is being assembled.

On September 18th, Carrie-Ann Talbot, from Pawtucket, was found after she was sexually assaulted and beaten in Roger Williams Park. For some reason, her attack concentrated on one eye, to the point where she lost sight. She was only 14 at the time. That alone makes you wonder how he went from the 58-year-old to the 14-year-old. Maybe due to his issues, any woman would do.

He and Carrie-Ann had smoked marijuana together. The theory was that he thought he finished the job and mistakenly walked away. Carrie-Ann would identify Raymond as a guy who tried to portray the role of "pimp."

The cops knew Lassor from the streets. At the time, they thought he might be responsible for another assault in his hometown of Westerly. Under interrogation, he signed off saying he committed all the murders and copped to the rape pretty easily.

His trial lasted almost two years from beginning to end. His court-appointed attorney spent all the trial attacking the teenage victim. Because he had already admitted to details that you wouldn't know unless you were there, the jury had no problem convicting him. He was the first person to be successfully prosecuted under the brand new "Life without Parole statute."

At the trial, "life without parole" actually made the family members of the victims the most happy. Some of them actually went on the record saying they were happy the crimes were not committed in a death penalty state. They were rather glad he would still be suffering as he is today.

JEANN LUGO

On June 24th, 2022, an abortion rights rally was being held in Rhode Island. Jennifer Rourke, a candidate for State Senate at the time, was protesting with many others. Jeann Lugo arrived, got grabbed by somebody, and then decided to punch Jennifer in the face. He was arrested for the act. Normally that would be the story but in this case, there were two overriding factors. He was also a candidate for the same seat. If that didn't twist things up enough, he was, and still is, a Providence Police Officer.

At trial, the judge ruled that Jeann had been grabbed and things were starting to turn up intensity wise. Therefore, the judge decided that Jeann was reacting in a "police manner." Yes, many of us wonder how the judge overlooked that it was a political rally that Jeann was opposing. Many of us wonder how the judge forgot that Jeann is a white male and Ms. Rourke is a black female. Many of us have not only started investigating the judge, we have tossed back and forth the idea of filing an "illegal in-kind contribution complaint" against the Providence Police Department. Every time we play the tape forward, as cool as this would be, we end up with more problems than we started with.

The next decision in Jeann's case happened in April of 2023. Would Jeann keep his job or not? Rhode Island is a state that has the Law Enforcement Officer's Bill of Rights (LEOBOR). Of course, after a hearing, he was allowed to keep his job.

JEANN LUGO

For me, both LEOBOR and his job as a police officer, unless we decide to file the campaign finance complaint, are immaterial. I have escorted young women into health care clinics. Sometimes they are only there for a cancer screening. The anti-choice types don't care. They've pointed guns at both the young ladies and me. Any clown who would punch a woman in the face at a rally is only a step away from that behavior.

I really don't want Jeann around any women at all. Has he abused other women in the past? If he was so comfortable with punching a woman at a pro-abortion rights rally, you know he will do worse when given the chance.

JULIO MERIDA

Julio Merida almost didn't make the list until I started doing the research. Yes, he's most wanted. Yes, he's old.

Back in 1987, there was a brawl at a soccer match. I can't even remember who was playing soccer in Providence in 1987. During the brawl, Mr. Merida and an associate shot and killed two people. Both were indicted the next year. It is believed they both fled to Mexico City. The case is so old, Rhode Island isn't even seeking federal assistance any longer. This is where it gets weird.

I reached out to some political friends from San Antonio, where my daughter was born in 1992, about connections they had in Mexico City. I have nothing outside of this. My only trips to Mexico City were before sobriety and in search of Ayahuasca, maybe a romantic escapade, and then back home.

It turns out there's this site called the Templo Mayor Museum in Mexico City. It was the location of a couple of Aztec Temples and therefore about 4,000 human sacrifices. Wherever there are sacrifices and executions carried out, ghosts follow.

Here's the weird part. In the last 20 years, according to folks familiar with what's going on, the "voices without bodies" have sometimes been speaking in English. Supposedly, some of the voices have reached out for a Salomon Martinez. That would be Mr. Merida's fake ID name.

I thought only Oliver Hazard Perry and Stephen Decatur traveled as ghosts. You learn something new each day.

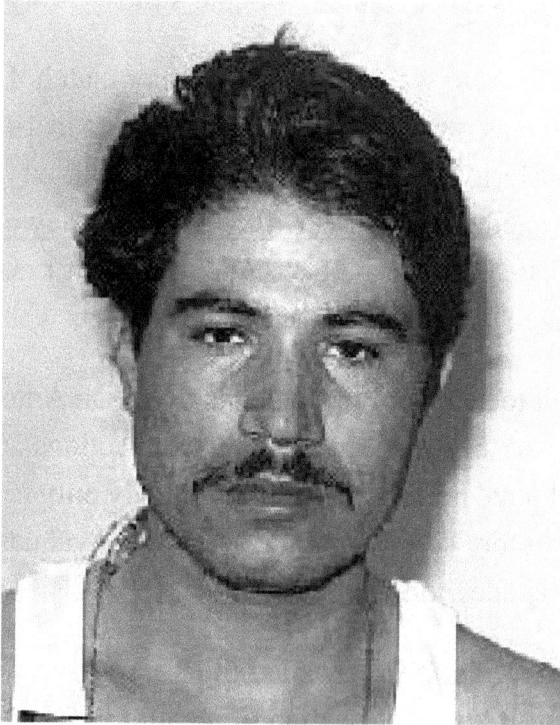

JULIO MERIDA

Is this real? Are people screwing with me? Well, here's the problem. If you lived in Mexico and didn't know Mr. Merida's alias, unless he told you personally, why would you run this out as a story? I can't wait to see where the universe takes this one.

STEPHEN MORIN

So if you commit crimes all over the country and end up getting executed, but can only brag about the crimes you committed here because you were never arrested for any of them, are you still a Rhode Island Rogue? Stephen Morin and I say yes. We love recognizing where he came from.

In 1951, he was born in Providence. He got the gene for addiction from somewhere. He discovered heroin at an early age and started skipping school. Before long, he added LSD to the mix.

During his teen years, he left Rhode Island for Florida. Warm weather and girls with less clothing can make you do that. This is especially true if you're feeding a heroin habit. Sleeping outside and in cars is a lot more comfortable in Florida than Rhode Island.

We know he's got a car theft in Florida. He's got a couple of rapes, depending on who you talk to, in North Carolina. In California, San Francisco to be exact, he upped his game to kidnapping, sexual assault, and rape. One woman spent 11 days with him after being abducted and being sexually assaulted multiple times each day. That makes me wonder if he's Bipolar 1 as I am. Not everybody shares a version of Manic Hypersexuality.

STEPHEN MORIN

After Texas, murder became the chief goal when he got to Nevada. He's been tested for possibly being involved there. He's been charged with 48 murders across 9 states. I've campaigned in 38 states and technically committed crimes in all of them due to my early cocaine preferences. But few are a match for this guy.

In Texas, the heroin really must have taken control because he started getting sloppy. He had to shoot two women because he couldn't abduct them properly. Many of us, the great majority with

Bipolar 1, like drugs that take us up so our "superpowers" increase. A small minority, Morin might have been one, go in the other direction to quiet all the noise. I used alcohol for that.

My daughter was born in San Antonio. I remember going back to the Sands Motel 11 years after Stephen was arrested there. I never would have put those together. Even stranger is that he was living with the woman he had abducted and another young lady. The Dru Valdes murder charge carried a capital offense. He had multiple other charges in Texas alone, and then other states starting showing up with other charges. He eventually pleaded guilty and was sentenced to death.

Before he received a lethal injection, a lengthy process in his case due to all the heroin use, he forgave everybody and then Stephen told God he would see him soon. Yes, some family members of those who were killed wished that he had been convicted outside of Texas. Some of them wanted him to be alive so he could suffer more.

There are a couple of things at play here. Folks taking LSD and heroin can't sexually assault somebody. Sexual assaulters and those of us with Narcissistic Personality Disorder usually start out with animals. There's no way Stephen starts his career in Florida without having done things in Rhode Island first. We should probably check some cold cases of assault and rape, since he may not have graduated to murder in 1961 and 1962. It's never too late for victims to receive justice.

Bobby Oliveira

CARLETON O'BRIEN

It's about time we had some order. Carleton O'Brien learned at an early age that he wanted to keep the family life and the criminal life separate. That would explain why he may have died the way he did.

He came up through the ranks of the independent gangster circuit not by doing "superstar" things, but by getting in hard work daily. He didn't want to be noticed. He did want to make a lot of money and feel safe, even with the chaos around him.

That may be why he developed a need for independence. He stayed away from the long-term deal and mafia relationship. A lot of folks thought he would just "walk away" at some point.

That was until he met Joseph Specs O'Keefe, who was always looking for that lottery ticket deal. He asked Carleton to help with a job. Carleton only wanted to be in on the planning and intelligence because he thought too much could go wrong, especially after the robbery was committed. He was right about that one.

On January 17, 1950, O'Keefe and his crew stole $2.775 million. Based on inflation, consider that to be about $35 million now. Once the robbery was over, all kinds of rifts in the group developed. Because Carleton was only in on the early part, he was saved from that. As large as the robbery was, the statute of limitations almost ran out before anyone was actually convicted.

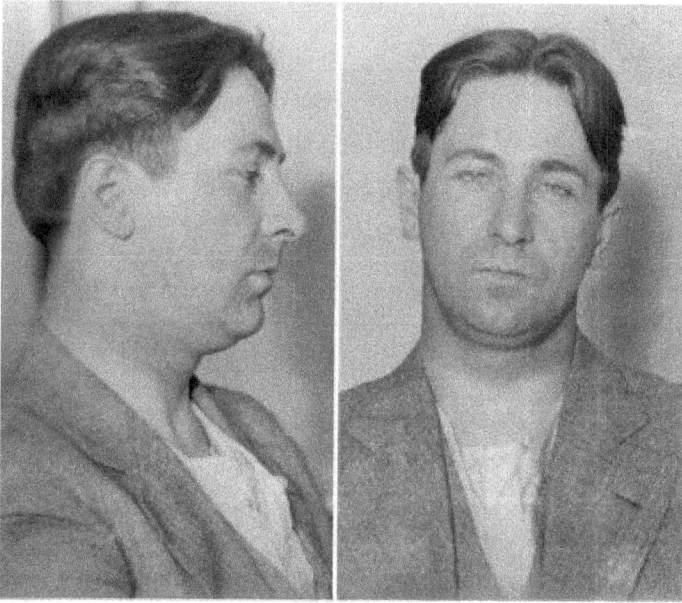

CARLETON O'BRIEN

In May 1952, Carleton's body was found. He had been shot and killed. Depending on who you believe, Carleton might have actually died in one of 3 places. It may have been in Pawtucket because of an affair, or it could have been in West Warwick or Cranston at properties he had an interest in.

The Patriarca crew wanted the local gaming operations all to themselves. Carleton was in the way. By killing him at home, they finally mixed his family and criminal lives together.

Carleton's last name, O'Brien, is meaningful to me because that was supposed to be my birth name. I was going to be Timothy Patrick O'Brien until I was given up for adoption. The O'Briens I was related to got thrown out of Ireland, thrown out of Boston, and thrown out of South Carolina.

The other weird thing about some O'Briens is they are always intermarrying with members of the Roche family. Know who has the name Roche in his family tree? Joe Biden does.

Time for some "Ancestry.com" or "23 and Me" research. Am I related to Carleton? Am I related to the President by birth? How much do I want to admit to?

GERARD OUIMETTE

Is it worse to be adopted, like I am, and know your parents are probably gone for good? Or is it worse to have to watch the family around you disappear, one at a time, at an early age? Gerard Ouimette went through the second one. That might explain a lot.

When Gerard was born, things looked good. Yes, he was one of eight kids, but daddy had a cool job as the Governor's chauffeur. He lived in an upscale neighborhood. One diagnosis made it all go wrong.

His dad contracted tuberculosis. That meant the chauffeur became a taxi cab driver. Then the taxi cab driver became a patient. When Gerard was 7, his dad passed away. The entire family had to move to Federal Hill. Suddenly, nuns are in and out of the house all the time providing charity.

Almost immediately, he was off and running. He and his brother hated being poor so they shoplifted together. At the age of 10, he got his first weapons charge after police found him in an alley with a weapon. He said he found it after the real thief discarded it. This incident sent him to the Sockanosset School for Boys. All he did the whole time he was there was fight. After almost a year, he returned home.

GERARD OUIMETTE

I suffer from Narcissistic Personality Disorder. I found out at age five when my parents sent me to a psychiatrist because I was doing serial killer things. He diagnosed me with this disorder. Each time I walk through Gerard's life, I wonder what may have happened if he had gotten help with his mental health. Then I discover the other things going on around him and I wonder whether it would have mattered at all.

He did see a psychiatrist at 18, but the doctor blamed most of his issues on a "lack of moral principles." That's almost like blaming mom and dad without blaming mom and dad. He did try to see if the Army would work, but he barely got out of basic training before getting tossed. He returned home and decided to engage in an armed robbery of a jewelry store before his 19th birthday. He would be sentenced to six years.

While he's in prison, his two eldest brothers get wrapped up in a construction accident and then die. When he's released, it only takes him six months to violate parole. Living with mom in East Providence didn't change the need to break the rules.

At this point, you have to wonder how much he values life. Everyone he loves finds a way to go through a crisis or die. Caring for people becomes so scary for some people that they would rather do anything else. The behaviors they engage in to accomplish that can be somewhat scary.

It was around this time that he meets a young lady and impregnates her. She is heavily Catholic. He has been telling friends since his brothers died that "There is no God." She wins out and doesn't have an abortion. The plan is that he will throw her cash once in a while.

A few years later, he will get invited to Raymond Patriarca Senior's, (always important to highlight the Sr. part) cigarette shop up on Federal Hill. Gerard has gone from upper middle class kid to neighborhood kid, to guy who has done time. They reviewed his talents and decided the best thing he could do is run the stolen car division. He will soon graduate. There will be another gun charge. While serving that charge, he will get accused of his first murder. We must remember that he's committed a few by now but this is the first time he gets arrested. He will eventually be found not guilty when a witness says Gerard wasn't there. However, his relationship to violence is carved in stone. You can see how death being "just something that happens" is part of his psyche.

According to what Gerard wrote in his memoir, it was local cops who came up with his nickname "The Frenchman." While they despised his actions, they seem to appreciate his style. They also loved pointing out that even though he grew up and learned his craft on the Hill, he wasn't Italian.

On July 9, 1972, he was still serving time for the gun possession charge. Michael Greene and Homer Perkins had been found dead three years earlier. Gerard was charged. He was found guilty and hit with another 10 years. He would serve that at the ACI. Who knew that 30 years later, I would get sober in the same building? (Yes, those of us who get sober in "jail" always wonder who served before us or, more importantly, who was serving with us that we didn't even know.)

Back in those days, the mob ran the North State Wing. They served there. They recruited there. They did deals there. Even though he was in jail, he was Patriarca Sr.'s second-in-command the entire time he was serving. Some will tell you he even had influence over prison management.

Gerard figured out that if he were part of the National Prisoners Reform Association (NPRA), he could get access to a phone. Yes, he would do his NPRA work but he could also do mob work as well. It wasn't too long before he had not only access to a phone but had one in his cell. This leads to the Vincent Vespia incident.

Vincent Vespia is a State Police Detective Sergeant. Gerard calls and threatens him. Much to Gerard's surprise, Vincent shows up at the prison, gets in Gerard's face, and rips the phone off the wall. Gerard will get charged over the threat but later acquitted.

Are you going to spend $2,000 on groceries this week? How often do you have friends over? Gerard regularly had John Gotti stop by. I guess Mr. Gotti was hungry because Gerard regularly had Italian groceries smuggled in to the tune of about $2,000 in today's money. To say he had total control of the place, with help from his associates, is an understatement.

When Gerard gets out, due to a reduced sentence, a couple of days before Halloween in 1977, things get a little weird. Some local mob types said that he was way too big for his britches. Problem one is he wasn't Italian and therefore couldn't be a "made" man. However, when they played the tape forward, killing him, as annoying and "out of place" as he was, created more problems than it solved.

Law enforcement at all levels wanted him. They figured he was responsible for eight gangland killings. They also knew they created internal distress anytime they mentioned Gerard as Patriarca Sr.'s "Number 2" because of the "but he's not Italian" thing. State Police Detective Brian Andrews started calling him the "Prince of Atwells Avenue" which he knew went up all the traditional Italian mobsters' backsides.

The FBI went so far as to say he had his own "Faction" equal to the Italian factions. They started spreading stories that "people who couldn't get made" would flock to the "Ouimette Faction." That all may have been out of frustration. At that time, Gerard was a suspect in every killing carried out by the mob. He was even charged a couple of times. He was always acquitted. Between not being found guilty and not being Italian, nerves had to be on edge everywhere.

Charles Kennedy, another non-Italian, had been one of his top Lieutenants in prison. In 1980, they had a falling out. Kennedy predicts Gerard's demise. When it doesn't happen right away, Kennedy has to try to cause it. You get the feeling some of Kennedy's crew were talking to the cops.

In 1981, a businessman gets killed mob style and Ouimette gets acquitted yet again. In 1984, he's in the middle of an assault at a cafe and the cops show up. This results in a weapons charge that gets him 18 years.

In 1994, he got paroled and moved to Fall River, Massachusetts. I was living there then, my refined cocaine product career would start four years later, and it was wild. You could always tell when he was going somewhere because of all the people following continuously. For some reason, about three or four months in, he puts together an extortion deal with Robert DeLuca. It will be a short amount of time before they get arrested in two different extortion scenarios. In one, it was six figures so the temptation made sense. The other one was only for $5,000.

Future Senator Sheldon Whitehouse was going assigned the trial as the US Attorney for Rhode Island. So much for omerta. Everybody shows up to testify against him. Not only everybody in his faction, but a bunch of folks from the non-Italian faction and a few entertainers from the Satin Doll, who had some interesting reactions while the trial was going on. Seems that people remember when you're really angry in public.

He was found guilty in late 1995 and on February 1, 1996, he was given life without parole due to the three strikes and you're out statute. He was the first New England criminal to get hit with that one. The only thing that Gerard could say in his defense was that the witnesses were "paid." Maybe he should have addressed the non-Italian thing?

In April 2015, at age 75, he died in a North Carolina prison due to heart disease and lung cancer. Two thirds of his entire existence had been spent in various prisons. Yes, in the words of the Rhode Island State Police, he was one of the "most notorious villains ever created."

However, isn't there more than that? Isn't this a story about separation and death and help not being provided? We should never excuse what he did. At the same time, shouldn't we do our best to make sure it doesn't happen again? If you know somebody going through something, please check in on them today

RAYMOND PATRIARCA, JR.

It's too bad we didn't have the term "Nepo Baby" back in the 1980s. It doesn't mean someone is entirely untalented. It does mean that their talent level is not what got them to where they are. Welcome to Raymond Patriarca Junior's world.

Daddy dies and suddenly there are all kinds of questions. First and foremost because the Senior version was so effective and cool. It is actually the Gambino family that is going to make the decision about who gets to lead next. As everyone knows, that always works out well.

In fairness to Ray Jr., things were indeed a mess when the Gambinos handed him the keys. In 1986, Rhode Island Supreme Court Justice Joseph Bevilacqua, Sr., was impeached. Some leaked FBI documents come out. Some have Ray Patriarca, Sr., making comments about "Italian women not telling on you if you smack them in the mouth." Ray. Jr. has to apologize and roll with "daddy never really said that." While that may have played with the general public, some misogynist members of the mob, the type to prefer transactional sex, found it to be weak.

In 1987, Larry Zannino went to jail and William Grasso became underboss. Now we have an inexperienced top boss and an underboss who just reacts without thinking things through. How much do you want to bet that Mr. Grasso was a transactional sex fan? Thankfully, the Genovese family solved that problem when they killed Grasso in 1989. This is when Nicky Bianco gets his time in the spotlight.

RAYMOND PATRIARCA, JR.

Sadly, both Ray, Jr. and Mr. Bianco are not detail oriented. This is how the FBI gets a tape of the induction ceremony. This was so embarrassing that even though it was partly Mr. Bianco's fault, he gets named boss. That would only last for a year since he'll be going to prison soon. A year later, Ray, Jr. will soon follow into prison.

Frank Salemme moves everything to Boston and creates a total mess. While that's a total mess, moving operational decisions back to Providence seems worse so it has never happened. Compared to what I grew up with, that's sad.

It will get worse. Ray, Jr. gets out of prison and "retires." Did he really retire or was he just not offered a contract? I know you want to say "But Bobby, that's awesome. All the real criminals are up in Boston now."

You could say that, but the problem is we have all the AAA types down here now. They do silly things like the Tidewater Landing Stadium debacle. They don't hide things well and it's not professional. Whenever they try to pull off one of their little scams, it's more insulting than scary. Raymond Patriarca Senior must have a lot to say on the other side. Maybe that's a cue to visit his grave. Sounds like a spiritual shave to me.

RAYMOND PATRIARCA, SR.

Sometimes when a cool person's name is mentioned, you can feel their presence. They don't have to do anything or even be there. The truly confident never try too hard. As kids, that's the way we all felt about Raymond Patriarca, Sr., even though he went to jail before we went to kindergarten.

Speaking of kindergarten, Ray, Sr., didn't make it through third grade. He left school at age eight to shine shoes and be a bellhop. In his teens, he's deeply involved in ignoring prohibition laws. Hijacking, assault, auto theft, safe cracking, and armed robbery are all going to be on the sheet.

Prohibition really guided the path he was on. The Providence Board of Public Safety would be referring to him as "Public Enemy #1" soon. He will catch an accessory to murder charge. Ray, Sr., was so good at what he did that he once convinced an attorney to create a priest who did not exist to advocate for his parole.

RAYMOND PATRIARCA, SR.

Each day in the 1940s, Ray, Sr., climbed a rung on the local mafia leadership ladder. Phillip Buccola got messed up in a tax evasion mess as 1950 rang around and Ray, Sr., had his chance. The coolest thing he did was move the whole operation to Federal Hill. I know I'm not supposed to, but I miss Coin-O-Matic. No matter what you did: bookie, sex worker, fraud, managers of the same, you paid a "tax." I wonder if those folks who steal the catalytic converters today pay a "tax"? Somebody should get on that.

Ray, Sr.'s, big play was to come up with something incredibly nasty to do, and then force them out of the state when they couldn't do the incredibly nasty thing like kill their own child. The fact that he took them down the road made everyone fear him. Non "creepy" murder was something he didn't mind carrying out. It's hard to calculate how many members of the Winter Hill gang offered to be killed in Boston because they were both fighting over turf for their loansharking markets.

He had a style where he didn't have to brag. He could point to the numbers and that would cause fear to happen. Throw in a little bit of inventiveness and he was everybody's favorite villain.

Why did he go to jail? Omerta got broken yet again. Red Kelley was ordered to kill Rudy Marfeo. Red gets sloppy. Red gets arrested. Red gives up Ray, Sr., and runs off to witness protection in 1970. Ray, Sr., gets hit with 10 years. Thanks to his management skills, he could still run things from inside the FBI. Later we will all find out that Red made a lot of it. Perjury plus braking Omerta has to be the worst.

One thing he couldn't control was his diet. He suffered from diabetes and heart disease for a long time. People close to him said trying to stay on the right path when it came to food was a struggle. Somehow he kept in shape, but internally things were a mess. He had a heart attack in the summer of '84. Even those of us who were underage drank in his honor. Then again, based on my history, if a character died on a soap opera, I drank in their honor.

Bobby Oliveira

CRAIG PRICE

How early does evil begin? When someone does something at the onset of puberty that is truly horrific, is that evil or just illness on display? Kindly meet Craig Price.

According to Craig, it might have even been revenge. He claims that as a child, a bunch of white folks hurled slurs at him. When that wasn't enough, they tied him up and threatened to run him over with one of their cars. Alexander Anderson would like a word.

We do know Craig had been arrested at 11 or 12 for petty theft. That sounds like kid stuff. What puts him on this list was not kid stuff. On July 27, 1987 – when he was almost 14 –he stabbed Rebecca Spencer 58 times. On September 1, 1989, when he was not quite 15, he stabbed Joan Helton 57 times. Was that supposed to be 58 and he lost count or was the first one supposed to be 58? Is there a significance to the numbers 57 or 58 in Craig's life?

He crushed her seven-year old's skull and stabbed her 10-year old 30 times. The stabbings were so severe that the handles of the knives broke and the knives themselves were found in the bodies. When Craig was arrested, he expressed zero remorse.

CRAIG PRICE

We have to ask some uncomfortable questions about the number of stabs. As someone who suffers from Narcissistic Personality Disorder, I know how sadistic tendencies can creep their way into sex. Were the stabbings sexual just based on the number? Did he talk to the victims while he was doing it? Did he get joy from each one, thinking, "I'm almost there, just one more"? Or was the whole thing a frenzy?

The problem with the frenzy theory is that at the time, he was taking marijuana and LSD. I went to Mexico City to take Ayahuasca and didn't go into a frenzy. Most folks on those drugs get spaced out and lazy. Thank God he didn't take meth – we could have lost a whole neighborhood.

Once he gets convicted, there's a hitch. At the time, regardless of what law you broke, you were supposed to be released at age 21. Craig used to brag about this possibility. Craig used to tell folks all the time that he was going to "make history."

Yes, laws were changed to prevent this occurrence in the future. Yes, advocacy groups did show up. What kept Craig in prison though was his need to get in trouble. Some conspiracy theorists who supported Craig getting out when he turned 21 – and they exist – think some of the trouble was "invented."

Yes, I was a building away from Craig while I was in the ACI in 2002. While I was going to my first AA meetings, he was still refusing psych evaluations, extorting and assaulting corrections officers, and getting into fights. Getting into fights was his favorite.

The violence in prison got so bad that he got shipped to Florida. Somewhere along the way, he became an expert at making home-made shivs. In 2017, he used one of the shivs to stab a Florida inmate and now it is guaranteed he'll be in prison until at least 2042.

This brings up a few questions. Will the violence in prison ever stop? Imagine if he had been released back in 1994. What other killings and criminal accomplishments would he have scored? What did he do before the age of 13 that we don't know about? Was this all pre-programmed or did he go from getting bullied to taking pleasure in over 50 stab wounds at a time? While the questions are uncomfortable, and until we learn to deal with them, the next Craig Price is right around the corner. Maybe they're stabbing someone 50 times as I type this. Maybe just down the street.

SERGIO SALAZAR-ASCENSCIO

Sometimes your criminal act creates an opportunity for somebody else to show off. That's what happened when Sergio Salazar-Ascenscio committed a murder in Providence. On that day in February of 2000, there was a dispute over a drug deal happening on Shiloh Street, which he settled with a gun.

He would finally be indicted in 2003. Of course the moment he got indicted, he took off. Seems to be a lot of that going around.

To this day, he is still on the run. He was born in Guatemala so that's always a possibility. As usual, New York City is on the possible "fled to" list, which I will get to in a second.

One of the things helping him is the number of Sergio Salazars and Sergio Salazar hyphen "anythings" that are out there. Just google the name. It's awesome to look at them all on voting lists.

Another thing I have heard but haven't been able to confirm is that he got tipped off. Somebody was in the grand jury room when his indictment came down. Somebody was really inside and got him a head start.

SERGIO SALAZAR-ASCENSCIO

It should be noted that David Rios also tried to run but failed. He helped commit the murder as well. In early 2005, David was arrested in Lebanon, Pennsylvania. Were he and Sergio still hanging out?

You know the FBI, since he crossed a state border, had to offer him a deal regarding Sergio's whereabouts. Sergio is still on the run, or dead - so David obviously didn't take the deal. In a weird way that makes me proud of him.

It should be noted that back when I would often get arrested during my addiction career, there was always an offer on the table about something else I might have known about. I never snitched because it goes against what I believe in. For the record, and in the interests of clarity, while I was in Utica, the FBI interviewed me a number of times about my Blog, especially regarding public records requests. They wanted to know how I found out what to ask for. In some cases I could tell them, "but it was available info," and in some cases I couldn't. They would also send along a note whenever they heard I got threatened. Nowhere in those interactions did I ever snitch on anybody.

In a weird way, the real rogue is David Rios. Willing to do more time because you respect the rules is something we should honor even if the original crime was reprehensible. Now you know why some New York City mafia types hate Donald Trump so much, but I never told you that.

FRANK SALEMME

Just because someone does many parts of a job well does not mean they are ready for a leadership position. In some cases, they do not have leadership skills and the whole thing falls apart. For just such an example, please meet Frank Salemme.

In the early days, he was talented. Frank grew up in Boston and was part of the gang wars. Whitey's crew knew who he was. On one trip to prison, he met a Patriarca associate and a new relationship began. Having a number of kills on your resume can do that.

Then the cracks started to appear. In 1968, Joseph Barboza was an informant. Frank was supposed to blow up Mr. Barboza's car. Frank kind of blew up the car and crippled Mr. Barboza but that wouldn't keep the witness from talking. He goes on the run until '72 and then gets convicted and does 17 years.

FRANK SALEMME

While he is away, the Boston and Providence factions are having an internal Civil War. On the Boston side is the Winter Hill Gang and Whitey. In early '89, Frank is released and it is clear he wants control. Joseph Russo had some control and wasn't in the mood for this. That is what led to the infamous IHOP shooting that summer. Things would continue raging back and forth until John Gotti showed up and put a deal together. Nicky Bianco would be boss, Russo would be consigliere. What that really meant is that Salemme was calling the shots.

This is where it gets cloudy. There's a film crew in the early 90's working in Rhode Island. They don't want to pay union wages. Some say that Frank's son, Frank Jr., pitched the idea of extorting cash from the film crew. Some say that's mafia white-washing and that Frank came up with it all by himself. That's what I was told when I was the Primary Field Coordinator for the Bill Clinton Campaign in '92 that put me on Federal Hill daily. No matter whose idea it was, it sucked because the film crew was actually the FBI. Fran tried to run but he got arrested in Florida.

This is where it starts to get murky. In 1994, the John Connolly trial was happening. Frank denies committing the murder of a nightclub owner. A couple of years later, Steve Flemmi, so much for Omerta again, can't wait to testify that Frank did it. When Frank goes to prison, he starts talking. Mr. Flemmi is also talking. They seem to be in a weird competition as to who can admit that they lie the most on behalf of prosecutors. Fellow inmates are tak-ing notes. Frank doesn't get charged with the murder of the night-club owner, but instead with perjury and obstruction. The plea deal is for time served.

A few years later, Frank finds out that Mr. Flemmi and Whitey have been cooperating for years. He wants in on the action. Once again, what happened to Omerta? The guy who Mr. Flemmi and Whitey gave the most info to? The retired FBI agent who arrested Frank in the first place. Not everybody gets to put their arresting agent in jail. Then again, not everybody violates Omerta. In 2003,

Frank would be released provided he testified before Congress.

In 2018, Flemmi and Whitey turn the tables once again. They testify that Frank had helped kill Steven Disarro back in '93. That would put Frank's body count in the high teens. In the Disarro case, Frank didn't do the murder. He indoctrinated his son by making his son kill Disarro while others watched. I guess Little League wasn't enough.

The question is, when did they all turn snitch? Was it as when reported or was this part of the game for a long time? By the time Frank gets done, the Rhode Island mob is a total mess. That is one of the reasons things are running out of Boston now. However, looking at what Whitey did, who is following in his footsteps? Frank would die quietly in prison in '22. His son, with leukemia from AIDS, had passed on in '95. Did that play a part in getting him to violate rule #1?

SAMUEL SLATER

"Wait a minute Bobby, how can Samuel Slater be a Rogue? He's responsible for the Industrial Revolution. Heck I'm wearing cotton clothes 'cuz of him. How can that be bad?" you ask.

This one depends on where you live. In the United States, we think of him as a successful American Industrialist. The person who established the first successful cotton mill in the United States – in our very own Pawtucket. In Britain, he's often seen as a traitor with no loyalty. He had a problem getting the gig he wanted in Britain so he pretended to be a farmer and escaped the country.

That's not all. He might have stolen some technology. Not just in the "Oh yeah, back home we did it like this" kinda way, but in an actual, "Before I answer that, let me roll out these plans I took from my boss's office" kind of way.

When he first got to the United States, he didn't like the cotton factories that offered him jobs. They used the old-fashioned, hand-driven models of manufacturing and he wanted to work with the newer, water-driven model. When he heard what Mr. Brown, of the firm Almy and Brown, was doing in Rhode Island, he saw nothing but opportunity. That brings up the next question. Did Mr. Slater actually work from memory as he designed the new machinery, or had he hijacked British plans which he then implemented at Mr. Brown's in the United States?

SAMUEL SLATER

There is a parallel in the technology world. Silicon Valley almost happened in Massachusetts. What stopped it from happening? Working for a tech company in Massachusetts, you had to sign a Non-Disclosure Agreement. But NDAs were illegal in California. It was only a matter of time before a number of folks migrated in the name of "intellectual freedom."

So is Mr. Slater a criminal, per se? Well, the whole "not being able to leave Britain thing" is troubling. He should have been able to do that. The bigger question that we'll never know the answer to is did he work with Mr. Brown based on memory or stolen documents? That one is a deeper question.

As is often the case when we talk about the various Rogues, perception matters. If you retired after working for a number of years in a US factory, you love him. If an ancestor became an indentured servant or a sex worker because suddenly England's factories weren't as competitive, he is the biggest criminal on the planet. You have to admit that leaving England with farmer's paperwork was pretty cool and one of the reasons why we like the criminal element in the first place.

RIGOBERTO VASQUEZ

So a drunk drives down the road. Somewhere in the middle of the street is a guy with Cerebral Palsy. Rigoberto Vasquez hits Gary Laramee, knocking him about 40 feet down the road. There is debris everywhere.

As luck would have it, it happens on Martin Luther King Day eve. It is also going to be Mr. Laramee's birthday. The next day, a Justice of the Peace sets bail at $100,000. At this point, Mr. Laramee is holding on so charges are limited. The next day, a judge reduces bail to $50,000 and Mr. Vasquez makes that with a review coming up on Friday.

Two days later, Mr. Laramee dies from his injuries. Charges are added including DUI Death Resulting. Do you think Mr. Vasquez shows up for his bail hearing? Of course not. He has been on the run ever since.

The first question is: shouldn't there be a way to put circuit breakers in the system when someone could die? I know, I know, Sunny Von Bulow is asking the same question – more on her later. However, based on the accident alone and the aftermath, didn't that tell somebody something?

RIGOBERTO VASQUEZ

I have heard from sources in the courtroom that members of the judge's staff had confided to members of the media that they thought it was going to get worse, but nothing could be done. No one is asking that an innocent man be held. We are asking that if someone might be guilty and the crime might become more serious in nature, that it be accounted for.

For the family, they remember the birthday celebration they didn't have the most. I've spoken to Michael Laramee. Literally each day he posts about his brother's passing. He is not the only family member who does so. They are not easy to read due to the realness of the emotional pain being expressed. I'm conditioned to absorb that in recovery meetings; outside in everyday discourse it hits so much harder.

Mr. Vasquez may have left the country. Even if he didn't, there are 734 folks with his name in 437 cities. That's before getting to undocumented people and non-voting citizens. That does not account for whether or not he uses an alias.

Let me be clear. I drove drunk over 5,000 times in my drinking career. I rolled three cars over. Thankfully, I only had a passenger once. She wasn't hurt. I needed stitches behind my ear, but didn't know until I showed up at a friend's house to use the phone. She screamed when she saw the blood running down my neck.

Thanks to a great lawyer, I have one OUI instead of a DUI. I should have had others, including that night when I was 19 driving the wrong way on Route 6 in Seekonk and the officer recognized that I was "so and so's nephew." He had me drive over to the Newport Creamery for a couple of cups of coffee instead of arresting me. I got lucky now and again. (Still not as good as Rob Morotti announcing "Rita's not going to like this" in an SMU Police Car one night, but that story has to wait for another book.)

Some irresponsible folks and many others deep in addiction are going to drive drunk. This isn't about that. This is about taking responsibility after the fact. I cannot imagine trying to stay sober knowing you killed someone and ran. The pressure and shame are too great.

Based on what we know about him, it could be Narcissistic Personality Disorder, but not likely. People have told me using substances for him was a regular deal. There is no way he got sober in the time since the accident. He is probably dead. Then again, sometimes the universe keeps people like him alive just to make a point.

ALEX VIGNIERO

Did Alex Vigniero get the nickname "Puto" because he was a prostitute or because he was gay? Was it some other incident and then someone tried to be funny? How many guys nicknamed "Puto" have committed murder?

We know Alex did. On March 7, 2008, just before he turned 30, that is exactly what happened. He committed murder where he was living on Waldo Street in Providence.

Even though he was an undocumented person, he had a Massachusetts ID. How did he get that? Could that be the "Puto" answer?

The wild part is while he is on a most wanted list in Rhode Island, there is no active investigation as to where he went. Did he go somewhere in Central America? Is he living somewhere as Luis Gonzalez-Caban, his favorite alias? Does April 17 have significance in his life or was that a random choice on the fake ID?

The lack of an investigation has raised a number of questions. The first one is, did he get a deal? Maybe being a snitch in the past earned him the nickname "Puto." If so, what else has he snitched about?

ALEX VIGNIERO

However, none of that got him on the Rogues of Rhode Island list; his ability to be an inspiration did. He accidentally caused some of the darkest "Bipolar 1" thinking I've ever engaged in. That will get you on the list.

On the day of the murder, he was driving a blue Nissan Maxima. The license plate was GT-373. The first question, not that dark, is well, anybody got that plate now?

"What's the darker version?" you ask impatiently. Imagine you hated someone. Imagine they were stolen from or even killed. Imagine you knew the license plate of the car the criminal was driving that day. Could you then, in celebration of the death, request that same plate as a vanity plate a year or two down the road? Just to keep alive the memory of what happened to them.

I called the Governor's Office regarding "preferred plates." They have not answered yet. I called the State Police. I think the questions unsettled them. They have not answered yet. I am probably going to have to file an APRA (that's a FOIA to the folks who do this nationally and a FOIL to the people who like to read what I write while in New York) to get the answer. Just for pushing this domino over, Alex deserves to be on the list.

CLAUS VON BULOW

Sometimes someone is cleared of all criminal charges and you still know they're up to something sneaky. This is true even when they're likable, even while doing obviously creepy things. That was how Claus Von Bulow lived his life.

Claus was actually born Claus Cecil Borberg. During World War II, his dad got accused of hanging out with the Nazis. Dad got cleared but Claus still decided his mom's name, von-Bulow, was the way to go. Claus will mess around with his legal practice in the fifties and then catch the gig of being assistant to J. Paul Getty. In June of 1966, he married Sonny, who happens to be the ex-wife of Prince Alfred von Auersperg. Think previous Austrian and Slovenian royal families on a third cousin level. Needless to say, he's in the right circles.

One day everyone wakes up and learns that Sunny Von Bulow is in a coma. How did that happen? The word insulin is being whispered everywhere. Claus gets arrested.

At this point, Claus has had a mistress for two years. Alexandra Isles seems to be known as having that role. She would testify at trial that there were heated arguments and long adult conversations about divorce, but no insulin. Seconal yes, without question; but insulin, no.

CLAUS VON BULOW

Back in 1982, my mom had not yet taken the job as assistant to the President at the Southeastern Massachusetts University Foundation, now known as the UMASS-Dartmouth Foundation. My mom was still involved in Coiffeur sur Mer, the salon she had opened with a friend. I was a private school kid so I would some days not go to school and hang around the salon a block from the courthouse, just to see who was coming and going.

That's how I first learned of Alan Dershowitz, as we all tried to see Cosima Von Bulow, Claus's daughter, as often as possible. For a 15-year-old kid, that was a big deal. As a married guy, I won't say anything else about Cosima. In any event, Claus was found guilty at the first trial.

There were two issues in question though. What was really in Sonny's system and how was some of the evidence obtained? Attorney Dershowitz would take over for the appeal.

This is where the "magic closet" comes into play. Supposedly, Claus had a closet he never opened where things were supposedly stashed. A private investigator hired by Sunny's family got onto the property and went through the closet in a fraudulent way. This involved telling a locksmith that the private investigators were part of the family and owned the property. Problem was anything from inside the closet had no connection to Sunny.

Attorney Dershowitz got the conviction tossed. Even people who loved Sunny were rooting for him back then. We had no idea he'd become a Trump supporter who thought 15-year-olds getting married was no big deal. Imagine the way you felt about Rudy Giuliani on 9/11 versus now.

Then at the second trial there was the issue of the medical record themselves. Attorney Dershowitz had a team of experts ready to testify that Sunny may have done a lot of things, but insulin was not one of them. One of the big giveaways is where insulin was on one of the "obtained" needles. It just did not match with how injecting someone with a substance works. There was also a previous incident where Sunny had ingested 73 aspirin tablets a few weeks before. Once again, Attorney Dershowitz wins and Claus is a free man.

After the second trial, Claus took off for Europe. However, he was always rumored to be back in town. I hate landscaping but when the opportunity came to join some of his buddies in cutting the lawn at Clarendon Court, I happily volunteered. In 1985, I was a tour guide at Astor's Beechwood. My jog would always get real slow when I went by the house. Yeah, he was innocent but you knew other things had to be up. As it turns out, Sunny would not die until 2008.

Then something weird started to happen. Some homeless people started witnessing a woman in a hospital gown, matching Sunny's appearance, wandering around Washington Square. The first question you had to ask is, "Wait a minute, Claus was guilty here and not guilty in Providence, shouldn't she be there?" Then again, Oliver Hazard Perry's ghost is in two buildings, like Stephen Decatur's, and now reportedly on a ship. Anything is possible, I guess.

In case you're wondering, yes, most homeless folks suffer from addiction and/or mental illness. That would be about 65 percent of them. However, when three homeless folks tell you the same stories about what they see on the streets at night, unprovoked by you and they all match, you kind of have to wonder. Recovery leads to wondering about ghosts; going to meet the ghosts leads to discovering things about criminals. Claus might have been innocent in this case but I'm hoping one of the ghosts clues me in to what else may have been up.

PINE GANG

Did you know there is a gang called the Members of Pine? I didn't. Does a guy who might have the nickname "Pest" or the nickname "Heavy and Done" usually have a tattoo proclaiming "Warrior" on his arm? Not usually. Jonathan Espinal has done all that.

On March 18 2011, he shot two people on Oxford Street in Providence. He was arrested, made bail, and then disappeared. His accomplice is in jail as we speak.

Disagreement over names seems to be one of his talents. Different organizations have different nicknames for him. Multiple people with his name and his description have been arrested in New York, more than once, and in Florida. However, law enforcement says that although the names, nicknames, choice of weapons, and descriptions match, it is not the same person.

PINE GANG

Law enforcement also cannot agree on where he went. Some claim the Dominican Republic, some claim New York, and some claim Florida. For all we know, based on his ability to have people who look like him do things for him, he might have moved back to Providence by now. Now I have to go learn more about the Members of Pine.

TWO OFFICERS

At the turn of the century, the world was very different. Two officers were out on the railroad tracks by Gorton's Pond in Warwick. One of them, John B. Gendron, had five years on the force in 1902. Out of the woods, somebody panicked and shot him. Officer Gendron died. His seven kids would never see him again.

First of all, why were the officers patrolling the tracks by the pond? What was the officer's killer hiding? Did the killer think the officer was somebody else? Did his fellow officer do the crime and make the story up? Because of these lingering questions, this anonymous killer – whomever it was – belongs on the list.

I've walked by that pond a lot, but now I'm going to take a lot more notice when I'm where the tracks used to be. The universe might send a message or two.

The whole thing was just senseless. If it happened today, it would be even worse. Yes, 23 percent of officers have issues that make us question their fitness for the force. Yes, officers commit a large amount of domestic violence. However, if you're not in the

23 percent because of a penchant for racism, bigotry, or the need for domestic violence, you deserve to be honored. Every officer deserves the benefit of the doubt until they display differently.

Officer Gendron left behind a wife and seven kids. I only know because my wife recently filed a police complaint about something that happened at work and I went with her to the station. I had never before noticed the monument to the fallen. That includes when I was there due to the false arrest Rep. Pat Serpa put together on behalf of a Trump supporter back in 2022. I beat the case. Then I thanked the cops for their professionalism. It wasn't their fault.

I'm going to go through all the officers mentioned on that statue. First, I will make sure they are not part of the 23 percent, then I will try to honor the sacrifice they made. In some way, I will try to honor the families too. We have to get back to a place where things aren't always in one corner but mixed together in the way the universe actually works.

THE RHODE ISLAND MOB

The Rhode Island Mob we have now is not the Rhode Island Mob we had when I was a kid in the seventies. A lot has changed and not for the good. Let's examine how we got here by first taking a look at what it's supposed to be like.

Even through college, I thought the Rhode Island mafia crew had its act together. Then came an important day in 1990. I had just gotten a job as a speechwriter for then Representative, and future Massachusetts Democratic Party Chair, Joan Menard (D-Somerset.) I had been working for her for about three weeks when I got a message from a secretary in another Office at the Statehouse, saying that I should report to a particular address on a Friday because someone "liked the work I was doing."

That someone was Whitey Bulger. The address was his garage. He just wanted to tell me he thought I had a "future in the business." Cool stuff.

The second time was up in Utica. I had been bickering back and forth with Rufus Elefante's daughter Angela. I got invited to stop by Frank Meola's garage. Frank hadn't done anything illegal in years. However, he took the time to explain to me how "the rules worked and what I should expect." The lessons were amazing. In Rhode Island, I had bought drugs from mafia guys, drank with mafia guys at strip clubs, even watched mafia guys "lobby" at the Statehouse – but I never got the inside view. Matching that inside view with history was one of the best political lessons I ever had. For those that try to tell the world that Frank is a bad guy, I will remind you that he was there for me when mania almost caused me to commit suicide.

TOSCAN SOCIAL CLUB IN PROVIDENCE

Oh, I need to back up and take a side-step on that one. When I was diagnosed as Bipolar 1, I thought that was good news because suicide was off the table. Until one night in 2017, while I was in hypomania, and the voices started saying, "Hey, you wanna be a writer right? You've written plenty of poetry. Think of Hemingway and the other guys you know. What do they have that you don't? That's right, you wanna be famous, you need a suicide . . ."

Thankfully, Dialectical Behavioral Therapy saved my life. Frank helped me and my then girlfriend, now wife, stay out of the financial weeds. All of these lessons made me look at the Rhode Island Mob more and more sideways. Yes, some mafia folks will make the main list. However, because Rhode Island is so messed up, there are some who won't quite make it. They will always be "outside looking in."

So back in the days of Gaspare Messina, things were going along. He had been a boss for about twice years, since Gaspare DiCola was murdered. However, he's not watching his p's and q's. That means Frank Morelli can put together a separate crew in Providence.

Along the way, the Boston and Providence crime families realized they would be better off together. They reunited just before Raymond Patriarca, Sr. came to power. More on him later. He got the throne on April 27, 1952, in Johnston. He then set up Coin-O-Matic and got the New York families to respect the Connecticut River as a boundary. He was part of the Commission and had an investment interest in two Vegas casinos.

In 1957, the Apalachin meeting happened in Upstate New York. He was there so he was arrested. In 1960, Robert Kennedy became the Attorney General and it got worse. He was indicted in 1967, convicted in 1969, and spent time in jail until 1974. It was never good again and every day was a struggle for him. He died in 1984.

RHODE ISLAND MOB

His son Ray Jr. had friends in the right spots, so he took over. Ray Jr. was doing such a lousy job that William Grasso had to show up in a supportive role. Grasso ends up getting murdered – women or gambling or politics, but he's still dead – and the guy who was indicted for the murder ends up in Grasso's old position. In 1990, Ray Jr. was indicted under RICO and in 1992 he pleaded guilty. That makes him worthy of his own spot, even though he strikes out a lot.

WILLIAM GRASSO

All of a sudden, there were a bunch of murders and arsons. Bodies were dropping at card games and hot dogs stands. Then there's a little bit of a civil war with an internal rival faction. When that ended in 2001, a person who I will mention later got to return the favor and testify against Whitey. So much for Omerta.

From 2001 until 2011, who is running things depends on the day. The power structure had definitely moved back to Boston. Anthony DiNunzio might have made a good boss, but instead, he decided to listen to the Gambino family and joined them in extorting strip clubs. That got him arrested.

His younger brother Carmen DiNunzio was in jail at this time. He got out in 2015. Because DiNunzio was worried about who might get indicted next, he couldn't pay attention to things in Rhode Island. That meant that John Conti had to resign because he was connected to something called Organic Bees. Just think of how embarrassing it must have been for the top mafia staffer at the Whitehouse to have to call it quits over a weed operation. Things haven't gotten much better.

CARMEN DINUNZIO

There is one other thing we have to gently talk about. There was a time when folks rooted for the Mob because they helped keep order. In most places, folks with mobster connections stay away from "political positions." In Rhode Island, those connected to the Mob – see Senator Ruggerio, Senator Ciccone who bragged about it, Mayor Lombardi, former Mayor Polisena – all took positions assigned by the Catholic Church even though they put D's in front of their names. No Democrat likes this wing of the Party. They do that because they have a deal with the local Providence Diocese. The Diocese helps them get elected by breaking campaign finance law and the politicians make pedophilia cases go away.

64 percent of Catholics are Pro Choice. We just turn our ears off at Mass, then we go about our way. In Rhode Island, due to political back stabbing and the need to protect pedophiles, many Catholics go to church out of state – one of the reasons so many churches have closed in recent years. Of course due to the deal, Senator Ruggerio's church stayed open. If you look at the economics and the number of parishioners going to Mass, it should have closed.

I'm certainly not rooting for organized crime but I wish things could get more stable on the political front. Boston and New York mob members don't play this game. Rhode Island could learn a lot from them.

MISSING PEOPLE

We have to be fair. It's not cool to do a book regarding criminals unless we take care of some of the victims first. Missing folks almost never receive justice because even murdered bodies provide more evidence than your favorite chair to watch TV in does. We should have a short chat about missing folks from Rhode Island, since it is the right thing to do.

Of course, when folks hear about missing people in Rhode Island, they automatically think of the **Rhode Island Mob**. However, it's not usually quite that simple. This is especially true if the person is mentally ill and does not desire to be found.

Danny Walsh was a bootlegger in the early thirties. Some believe he went missing because of the mob. Some believe he went missing to avoid the mob. He was last seen at the **Bank Cafe in Pawtuxet**. His brother got a ransom note and went to pay it, but not even a corpse came back. Theories ranged from cement off Block Island to a shallow grave in Pawtuxet. They did excavate his house and find a body, but it wasn't his.

Frank Mazzella left his apartment in Westerly on February 7, 1999. He never returned. All of his personal belongings and his car remained behind. No blood, no ransom, no anything.

FRANK MAZZELLA

Donald Joseph Connell was a Marine who walked out of his house in Newport in 1986. Professionals wondered who he could have interacted with, based on the shape he was in at the time. His remaining family members still wish to find him.

Stefan Marfeo came back to an empty home in 1990. His wife **Doreen Marfeo** was missing, as was $600. However, all of her belongings were still there and nothing seemed to be out of order. Then things get weird. Turns out **Doreen** had been acting like she was heading towards a psychotic break. While that was going on, **Stefan** had her followed. Then two mystery letters show up at the local police department. One says Doreen is living a double life. The other says Stefan is responsible. Some years later, Stefan will get jealous over a new girl. He will end up killing someone and committing suicide. In the note, he says he feels guilty about what happened to Doreen, without saying he hurt her. But her body still hasn't been found.

Charlotte Lester was the story of last year and she's still missing. She was last seen in the **Apponaug** area of Warwick. Her car was found at **Kent County Hospital**. One particular talk show host thinks this has something to do with a gentleman who is being investigated for drug dealing. I think it's a right church, wrong pew kind of thing. Where she was last seen is close to a drug drop off spot. Right next to that is the **Remington House Inn**, where I have witnessed homeless activity. A quick walk over and looksee indicated the property is breachable. My guess is that she got involved with the drug running types and they deposited her where she was easy to hide. The big problem is the inn is in the middle of a tax fight, so getting the owners to allow folks to search has been almost impossible. Obviously if you have any information, please contact local authorities. I talk to my Higher Power daily about Ms. Lester. Prayers can't hurt and we hope the families of these folks can find closure.

LAST OF ROGUES

As always at this point, I make an apology. I know when you get done reading, I may have left out one of your favorites. It's just not possible to satisfy everybody, but I tried the best I could. You will also notice that I have my own set of things that makes it more likely for someone to make the list. Addiction is the easy one to spot. Sadism, because Narcissistic Personality Disorder causes that, is the other one. In anything I write, you start showing those traits and you will get some attention.

Sadly, the number of people who suffer from things like this and live long lives is incredibly small. For instance, using me as an example, walk up to a shrink and say, "All right, the patient suffers from addiction, Bipolar 1, OCD, Borderline Personality Disorder and NPD. What's the most likely outcome?"

The doctor will say, "Probably dead by suicide in their late thirties." People with my stuff aren't expected to ever stay sober. Living this long is a fantasy. That's why I feel the level of gratitude I do and express it by walking in cemeteries every Sunday.

If you know someone struggling, please encourage them to get help. If you reach out to one of us in the recovery community, we will happily try to help them turn around. If our combined efforts are successful, they will live incredible lives. This is especially true if they are young. I started drinking at 10 and doing coke at 12. If I wasn't a spoiled brat, I totally would have been more of a criminal than I was. Yes, a lot of my "crimes" were political backlash I escaped, due to great lawyers. However, early on in life, it wasn't like that.

If I get sober even four years before I do, I'm a millionaire now. Well, that's provided I survive. If I find out I'm Bipolar a year before I do, I don't have to go through that seven-day adventure with no sleep at all. Knowing I had to go through it anyway, I'd take my chances.

Sobriety diminished by NPD. Then it allowed me to learn how to manage my Bipolar 1 disease. While Bipolar is expensive when you go on an adventure, OCD is expensive every day. It keeps you from completing all kinds of tasks. Meeting my birth family meant a lot of the OCD disappeared, and now some things have happened that never would have otherwise, including this book.

After all that, if you still think I really missed out on somebody, please let me know. That could be the inspiration for another project. You could tell everyone you know it was your idea.

AUTHOR BIO

Bobby Oliveira is the Treasurer of the Quahogs United PAC and the creator of the Quahogs United Blog. He has more than 40 years of campaign experience, more than 35 years of sales experience, including from 2007-2011 when he was Sales Director at the Newport Bay Club until he sold out the inventory, and 30 years of writing experience going back to his time as a newsman at WHTB Radio and moving on to become the head speechwriter to future State Senator and Democratic Chair Rep. Joan Menard.

Mr. Oliveira has campaigned in 38 states. Most of this experience was garnered when he worked on Presidential campaigns in 1988 and 1992. He is a veteran of multiple New Hampshire Presidential Primaries.

Along the way, he has also served on teams that have been successful lobbying for laws and ordinances in 4 states. Due to that experience, he is a go to for various forms of public records requests including APRAs, FOILs, and FOIAs. When not doing that, he is often tasked to write radio commercials. He has done that for candidates at the municipal, county, state, and Federal levels.

Most memorable of those experiences happened back in the mid-90's. Dr. Irving Fradkin, of Dollars for Scholars fame, asked Bobby to change the city of Fall River's motto from "We'll try" to "Scholarship City". Thanks to Bobby's leadership, the City of Fall River's City Council voted in the affirmative for the change.

His sales career started in real estate rentals. From that, he had a 10 year career in floorcovering. Back in 1999, he secured the contract for the floorcovering in the Pfizer labs in Groton, Connecticut. In 2000, he was recruited by a timeshare firm and went on to have a 16 year career in timeshares and vacation clubs. He still sells ads for his blog from time to time. He has sold those products in 5 states.

While he has created political change and profit all over the country, he is most proud of his over 20 years clean and sober. He regularly works with newcomers so they can find the same peace he has. While he has a number of mental illnesses, he is able to manage 24 hours at a time. As a result, he has been asked to speak on addiction issues in the same number of states he has campaigned in.

As this is being written, Bobby has recruited a lawyer to represent Rhode Island's homeless camped out at the State House against an illegal eviction order the Governor brought forward. So far the combination of legal resources Bobby has brought together has beaten the Governor twice in court. Bobby hopes this will draw attention to the real services the homeless need especially regarding addiction and mental illness issues.

EPILOGUE

Analyzing the impact of organized crime on the state of Rhode Island over the past 50 years presents a complex narrative deeply intertwined with the state's history, economy, and social fabric. Rhode Island, though small in size, has not been immune to the influence of organized crime syndicates.

Origins and Evolution of Organized Crime in RI

Organized crime in Rhode Island traces its roots back to the early 20th century, coinciding with the rise of the Italian American Mafia in the United States. The Mafia, also known as La Cosa Nostra, established a foothold in Providence and other major cities in Rhode Island during the Prohibition era. Gangs controlled illegal gambling, bootlegging, and other vice-related activities, exploiting the demand for illicit goods and services during this period.

One of the most notorious figures in Rhode Island's organized crime history was Raymond Loreda Salvatore

Patriarca, Sr., who rose to power as the head of the New England Mafia in the 1950s. Under Patriarca's leadership, the Mafia expanded its influence across Rhode Island, Massachusetts, and Connecticut, engaging in a wide range of criminal enterprises, including extortion, loan sharking, drug trafficking, and racketeering.

Notable Figures and Activities

The Patriarca crime family, based in Providence, dominated organized crime in Rhode Island for decades. Besides Raymond Patriarca, Sr., other prominent figures included his son, Raymond "Junior" Patriarca, and underbosses Francis "Cadillac Frank" Salemme and Luigi "Baby Shacks" Manocchio. These individuals wielded considerable power and influence, controlling various illegal

LUIGI MANOCCHIO

operations while maintaining a facade of legitimacy through front businesses and political connections.

Illegal gambling remained a lucrative venture for organized crime in Rhode Island, with the Mafia operating underground casinos, sports betting rings, and numbers games throughout the state. Additionally, the trafficking of narcotics, particularly heroin and cocaine, contributed significantly to the crime syndicates' wealth and power. Extortion and loan sharking were also prevalent, with businesses and individuals coerced into paying "protection" money to avoid violence and retribution.

FRANK SALEMME

Raymond Loreda Salvatore Patriarca Sr., commonly known as Raymond Patriarca Sr., exerted a significant but often discreet influence on the politics of Rhode Island during his reign as the head of the New England Mafia. While Patriarca himself rarely directly involved himself in political affairs, his organization's pervasive presence and control over various illicit activities inevitably intersected with the political landscape of the state. Here are some ways in which Patriarca Sr. impacted Rhode Island politics:

RAYMOND PATRIARCA, SR.

1. **Corruption and Bribery**: The Patriarca crime family, under Raymond Patriarca Sr.'s leadership, was known for its ability to corrupt public officials through bribery and extortion. Politicians, law enforcement officers, and other government figures were sometimes compromised

by their associations with organized crime, either through direct financial transactions or implicit understanding of the consequences of crossing the Mafia.

2. **Influence Peddling**: The Mafia's control over certain industries and businesses allowed them to wield influence over policymakers and decision-makers. Patriarca Sr. and his associates could leverage their connections in construction, waste management, and other sectors to sway government contracts, zoning decisions, and regulatory policies.

3. **Vote Manipulation**: While direct evidence of vote manipulation by the Mafia in Rhode Island may be limited, there have been allegations and suspicions of organized crime involvement in electoral processes. Patriarca Sr.'s ability to intimidate and coerce individuals, combined with his network of loyal associates, could potentially have been used to influence local elections and political outcomes.

4. **Political Protection**: Some politicians and public officials may have turned a blind eye to the activities of the Mafia in exchange for favors or protection from retribution. The fear of retaliation from organized crime figures could dissuade law enforcement agencies and prosecutors from aggressively pursuing investigations into political corruption or criminal activity linked to the Mafia.

5. **Legitimizing Criminal Enterprises**: Patriarca Sr. and his associates legitimized their criminal enterprises by investing in legitimate businesses and cultivating relationships with influential individuals in the business and political spheres. This strategy allowed them to operate with relative impunity while maintaining a facade of respectability.

Overall, Raymond Patriarca, Sr.'s impact on Rhode Island politics was characterized by a combination of covert influence, intimidation tactics, and strategic alliances. While he himself may not have held formal positions of political power, his ability to manipulate and exploit the political system for the benefit of the Mafia cannot be underestimated. The repercussions of his legacy continue to reverberate in the state's political landscape, serving as a reminder of the insidious influence of organized crime on democratic institutions.

Impact on the Economy

The presence of organized crime in Rhode Island has had a detrimental impact on the state's economy and business environment. Legitimate enterprises faced pressure from mob-controlled rackets, leading to economic distortions and reduced competitiveness. Small businesses, in particular, were vulnerable to extortion and predatory lending schemes, stifling entrepreneurship and hindering economic growth.

Moreover, the infiltration of organized crime into industries such as construction and waste management inflated costs and compromised the quality of public projects. Bid rigging, bribery, and kickback schemes became commonplace, eroding trust in government institutions and undermining public confidence in the rule of law.

Law Enforcement Efforts and Responses

Law enforcement agencies at the local, state, and federal levels have waged a relentless battle against organized crime in Rhode Island. The Rhode Island State Police, in conjunction with the FBI and other federal agencies, conducted numerous investigations targeting Mafia leaders and their associates. The use of wiretaps, undercover operations, and witness cooperation played crucial roles in dismantling criminal enterprises and prosecuting key figures.

One of the most significant blows to organized crime in Rhode Island came with the federal prosecution of Raymond "Junior" Patriarca and other high-ranking members of the Patriarca crime family in the early 1990s. Racketeering charges resulted in lengthy prison sentences for several defendants, weakening the Mafia's grip on the region and paving the way for new leadership within the criminal underworld.

Sheldon Whitehouse, during his tenure as the United

States Attorney for the District of Rhode Island from 1994 to 1998, played a significant role in the federal efforts to combat organized crime in Rhode Island. Whitehouse pursued aggressive prosecution strategies aimed at dismantling the Patriarca crime family and other criminal organizations operating in the state. Here are some key aspects of Whitehouse's efforts to stop organized crime in Rhode Island:

1. **Racketeering Prosecutions**: Whitehouse's office targeted members of the Patriarca crime family and their associates through the use of federal racketeering laws. Racketeering charges allowed prosecutors to go after not only specific criminal acts but also the broader criminal enterprises and conspiracies orchestrated by organized crime groups. By charging individuals with racketeering offenses, Whitehouse aimed to disrupt the hierarchical structure and illicit activities of the Mafia in Rhode Island.

2. **Collaboration with Federal Agencies**: Whitehouse collaborated closely with federal law enforcement agencies, particularly the Federal Bureau of Investigation (FBI), to gather intelligence, conduct investigations, and build cases against organized crime figures. The joint efforts of the U.S. Attorney's Office and federal agents enabled the prosecution of high-ranking members of the Mafia and their associates on a range of criminal charges, including extortion, money

laundering, and drug trafficking.

3. **Use of Informants and Wiretaps**: Whitehouse's office relied on informants and wiretaps to gather evidence against organized crime syndicates. Informants provided crucial insider information about the activities and inner workings of the Mafia, while court-authorized wiretaps allowed investigators to intercept and record incriminating communications among criminal associates. These investigative techniques were instrumental in uncovering criminal conspiracies and obtaining convictions in court.

4. **Asset Forfeiture**: Whitehouse pursued asset forfeiture actions against individuals convicted of racketeering and other organized crime offenses. Asset forfeiture allowed the government to seize and forfeit assets acquired through illegal activities, such as money obtained from extortion, drug trafficking, or fraud. By depriving organized crime figures of their ill-gotten gains, Whitehouse aimed to disrupt their financial networks and deter others from engaging in similar criminal conduct.

5. **Public Awareness and Education**: Whitehouse recognized the importance of raising public awareness about the threat of organized crime and the efforts to combat it. He frequently spoke to the media and community groups about the work of his office and the need for cooperation between law enforcement and the public to address organized crime.

By engaging with the community and fostering trust and cooperation, Whitehouse sought to mobilize support for law enforcement efforts and enhance public safety.

SHELDON WHITEHOUSE LEFT A LEGACY OF LAW ENFORCE-MENT EFFECTIVENESS AND PUBLIC SERVICE IN THE FIGHT AGAINST ORGANIZED CRIME IN RHODE ISLAND.

Lasting Effects and Contemporary Challenges

While law enforcement successes have disrupted traditional organized crime networks in Rhode Island, the legacy of their influence persists in certain sectors of society. Street gangs and independent criminal organizations have filled the void left by the decline of the Mafia, perpetuating violence, and criminality in urban communities. Drug trafficking remains a persistent problem, fueled by the opioid epidemic and demand for illicit substances.

The allure of organized crime continues to attract individuals seeking wealth and power outside the bounds of conventional employment. The evolution of technology has facilitated new forms of criminal activity, such as cybercrime and identity theft, presenting novel challenges for law enforcement agencies maintaining public safety and security.

In conclusion, organized crime has left an indelible mark on the state of Rhode Island over the past 50 years, shaping its economy, culture, and law enforcement landscape. While significant progress has been made in combating traditional Mafia syndicates, the fight against organized crime remains an ongoing struggle. Vigilance, cooperation among law enforcement agencies, and community engagement are essential in addressing the root causes of criminality and safeguarding the future of Rhode Island.

The federal prosecution of the Mafia in Rhode Island was led by various law enforcement agencies and prosecutors over the years, but one notable figure associated with this effort was United States Attorney for the District of Rhode Island, Sheldon Whitehouse. Whitehouse served as U.S. Attorney from 1994 to 1998 and played a key role in prosecuting members of the Patriarca crime family and dismantling their criminal operations in the state.

During his tenure, Whitehouse oversaw several high-profile cases targeting organized crime figures, including

Raymond "Junior" Patriarca and other top-ranking members of the Mafia. These prosecutions were part of broader federal efforts to combat racketeering, extortion, and other illegal activities associated with the Patriarca crime family in Rhode Island and throughout New England.

Whitehouse's leadership and coordination with federal law enforcement agencies, such as the FBI and the Department of Justice's Organized Crime and Racketeering Section, were instrumental in securing convictions and dismantling the Mafia's influence in the region. His tenure as U.S. Attorney marked a significant chapter in the ongoing battle against organized crime in Rhode Island, leaving a lasting impact on law enforcement efforts and the state's criminal justice system.

Rogues of Rhode Island

www.ingramcontent.com/pod-product-compliance
Lightning Source LLC
Chambersburg PA
CBHW070758290326
41931CB00011BA/2059